English
National
Opera
Guide

8

Der
Rosenkavalier
Strauss

English National Opera
receives financial
assistance from the Arts
Council of Great Britain
and the Greater London
Council.

Lotte Lehmann as the Marschallin.

Preface

English National Opera Guides are companions to opera in performance. They contain articles and illustrations relevant to any production as well as those mounted by English National Opera. Of interest to all opera-lovers, also, is the complete original libretto of the opera, side by side with an English translation. There are many reasons why sung words may not be clearly distinguishable, whatever the language and however excellent the performance. The composer may have set several lines of text together, for instance, or he may have demanded an orchestral sound through which no voice could clearly articulate. ENO Guides give English readers the opportunity to know a libretto in advance and so greatly increase their understanding and enjoyment of performances whether live, broadcast or recorded.

ENO is very grateful to Mobil for sponsoring this *Der Rosenkavalier* Guide, as part of its wide-ranging programme of support for the arts. Such sponsorship is an indication of a steadily growing public interest in opera, and we hope the Guides will prove useful to new and experienced opera-lovers alike. An audience which knows what to look and listen for – one that demands a high standard of performance and recognises it when it is achieved – is our best support and, of course, an assurance for the future of opera in the English-speaking world.

Nicholas John
Editor

8

Der Rosenkavalier

Richard Strauss

*English National Opera Guides Series Editor:
Nicholas John*

This Guide is sponsored by Mobil Oil Company Limited

John Calder ● London
Riverrun Press ● New York

New York, NY 10010

© English National Opera, 1981

An Introduction to 'Der Rosenkavalier'
© Derrick Puffett 1981

Comedy for Music
© Michael Kennedy 1981

Hugo von Hofmannsthal — Man of Letters
© Peter Branscombe 1981

English Translation of Der Rosenkavalier by Arthur Kalisch
© Copyright 1911, 1912, by Adolph Fürstner.
Copyright assigned 1943 to Boosey and Hawkes Ltd for all countries except Germany,
Danzig, Italy, Portugal and USSR (in the boundaries of 1935).
Reprinted by permission of Boosey and Hawkes Music Publishers Ltd for the above
mentioned territory.

BRITISH LIBRARY CATALOGUING IN PUBLICATION DATA

Der Rosenkavalier – (English National Opera Guides; 8)
    1. Strauss, Richard. Rosenkavalier
    2. Operas – Librettos
    I. Strauss, Richard II. Hofmannsthal, Hugo von
    III. John, Nicholas IV. Series
    782.1'092'4   ML410.S93

ISBN 0-7145-3851-5

Typeset in Plantin by Margaret Spooner Typesetting

Printed by The Hunter Rose Company Ltd., Toronto, Canada

Contents

List of Illustrations

An Introduction to 'Der Rosenkavalier'

Derrick Puffett

In Iris Murdoch's novel *The Black Prince*, the narrator goes to a performance of *Der Rosenkavalier*. 'The curtain suddenly fled away to reveal an enormous double bed surrounded by a cavern of looped-up blood-red hangings... two girls were lying in a close embrace. (At least I suppose one of them was enacting a young man.) Then they began to sing... The two women were conversing in pure sound, their voices circling, replying, blending, creating a trembling silver cage of an almost obscene sweetness... these were not words but the highest coinage of human speech melted down, become pure song, something vilely almost murderously gorgeous... I was definitely going to be sick.'

Any newcomer to *Der Rosenkavalier* may experience some–one hopes, not all!–of these sensations. In the novel, it is true, they are not produced exclusively by the music; but Murdoch's language–'an almost obscene sweetness... vilely almost murderously gorgeous'–captures the work's immense physical power, its ability to attract and repel. What *is* it, this astonishing mixture of sentimentality and voluptuousness, of coarse good humour and tender naivety, of manners 'wholly Viennese' (Hofmannsthal) and emotions familiar to all? After an orchestral prelude which is probably music's most graphic depiction of lovemaking–Strauss tried to surpass it in *Arabella*, but there the music is not so good–he gives us not only Octavian and the Marschallin but Ochs, Sophie, Faninal, an Italian intriguer and his

Anne Evans (the Marschallin) and Josephine Barstow (Octavian). (photo: John Garner)

7

accomplice (not to mention Ochs's lackeys, ancestors of Macheath's thugs in *The Threepenny Opera*), the Three Noble Orphans, waiters, musicians and pantomime trapdoors. All in music ranging from pastiche rococo (Ochs's first entry) to pastiche Expressionism (his humiliation) and taking in, between the two extremes, the various types of music associated with Octavian, Sophie and the Marschallin.

First some cold facts. Strauss met Hofmannsthal in 1900; but their collaboration did not begin until five years later, when the poet approached the composer with the idea of turning his play *Elektra* into an opera. As they worked together, Strauss's respect for Hofmannsthal grew: 'We were born for one another', he wrote. Even before the *Elektra* première, which took place on January 25, 1909, they were discussing future projects. At that time Hofmannsthal was preoccupied with French literature of the 17th and 18th centuries; also with the characters of Mozart's *Figaro*. Then on February 11 he sent Strauss the 'scenario for an opera, full of burlesque situations and characters, with lively action, pellucid almost like a pantomime . . . It contains two big parts, one for baritone and another for a graceful girl dressed up as a man, à la Farrar[1] or Mary Garden[2]. Period: the old Vienna under the Empress Maria Theresa'.

This was the nucleus of *Der Rosenkavalier* (or *Ochs von Lerchenau*, as they came to think of it: the title was changed only four months before the première). Work advanced rapidly, and soon Hofmannsthal suggested: 'Do try and think of an old-fashioned Viennese waltz, sweet and yet saucy, which must pervade the whole of the last act'. The last act, as we know, was the one that gave Strauss the most problems; for whereas he was able to compose the music for the first two almost concurrently with the writing of the text (with some reshaping in the case of the second, it is true), he received the words for Act Three over a much longer period and thus had a correspondingly less secure grasp of the total shape. One reason for the delay was that Hofmannsthal was worrying about the character of the Marschallin. As she increased in importance, the work lost some of its intended lightness, and so (to paraphrase Norman Del Mar, author of the standard English study of Strauss) the 'Pantomime with opportunities even for a short ballet' turned into 'gay, cheerful, but profoundly psychological drama'. Once Strauss had the full text, however, composition proceeded swiftly. The première, a brilliant success, took place on January 26, 1911 at the Dresden Court Opera.

*

Four months later, on May 18, Mahler died (he had been brought back ill from New York without having heard the new opera). Strauss wrote to Hofmannsthal: 'Mahler's death has been a great shock to me'. At around the same time he wrote in his diary: 'I want to call my *Alpine Symphony* the "Antichrist", for it portrays moral purification through one's own strength, freedom through work, and worship of eternal, glorious nature!'

What do these remarks mean? That Strauss had been reading Nietzsche, to be sure, but what else? They sound unlike Strauss, somehow; more like Mahler—the Mahler of the letters or the Third Symphony. And freedom from what? Strauss had met Mahler in 1887, when both were in their twenties. From then until Mahler left for America (1907) their work brought them into

---

1. Geraldine Farrar (1882–1967), American soprano who made her début at the Berlin Court Opera in 1901.

2. Mary Garden (1874–1967), Scottish soprano who created the rôle of Mélisande in Debussy's *Pelléas et Mélisande* in Paris in 1902.

occasional contact with each other. According to Del Mar, Strauss's opinion of Mahler was typical of the time: 'That's really no composer at all. Just a very great conductor'. But his music suggests otherwise. In the early tone poems, notably *Don Quixote,* there are passages which may well have influenced Mahler, but after about 1900 the influence seems to be going the other way. Two Strauss works in particular, *Symphonia Domestica* and the *Alpine Symphony* (the latter not finished till 1915), suggest a musical obsession with Mahler; apart from the many cross-references, they were his last and longest tone poems and the only two to be called 'symphony'. Surely with two such near-contemporaries, both composer-conductors working in related fields of instrumental music, there must have been feelings of rivalry? Can one not detect in Strauss's diary entry, written in reaction to Mahler's death, even some spirit of relief?

Even during Mahler's lifetime, however, Strauss had, so it seems, tried to free himself from the other's influence, mainly by moving out of their common field: in opera Mahler could influence him only as a conductor. There is little Mahler in *Salome* or *Elektra*; on the contrary, Strauss's imagination seems to be burning more brightly than ever. But between *Elektra* and the *Alpine Symphony* comes *Rosenkavalier.* The opera is less obviously affected by Mahler than the symphonies, as we should expect. But there are two passages—and they are two of the most famous—which seem to me profoundly Mahlerian: the passage in which the Marschallin describes how she gets up at night and stops the clocks (harp harmonics, a favourite Mahlerian sonority), and the passage concerning her Uncle Greifenklau. It is interesting that both passages serve to suggest a dimension beyond the immediate dramatic context. The idea of 'time standing still' was to become a preoccupation, almost a cliché, with the composers of the next generation, composers such as Berg and Schreker; their works show they remembered this passage musically too. And the whole point about Uncle Greifenklau, the sick old man whom the Marschallin visits, is that he never appears in person: he is used to evoke a whole world of social interaction, a world which by its very nature cannot be represented on stage. The string theme, half-lamenting, half-aspiring ('one eye wet, one dry!' as Strauss told a singer), which accompanies the Marschallin at this moment is intensely Mahlerian: one wonders whether Uncle Greifenklau was not also Director of the Vienna Court Opera.

Now why all this Mahlerising? Because I want to get nearer to what *Rosenkavalier* is, and one way of doing this is by showing what it is not. For whatever else it is, it is not 'staged tone poem'—a cliché often applied to *Salome* and *Elektra.* This cliché seems to go back to Ernest Newman, but survives in all sorts of places, even the *New Grove,* which goes so far as to call *Salome* 'a tone poem with vocal interludes'. It is misleading, on one hand because it means ignoring the drama, on the other because it implies a false idea of what the tone poem had become. 'Symphonic writing', after Mahler, means a breakdown of the music into motifs, a constant variation of these motifs and an aural explanation of how these things are done, the last being provided through the orchestration—which thus becomes a more essential part of the composition than ever before. The orchestration in fact *is* the composition. Now as soon as we compare Mahler and Strauss in any detail we see that they are not really similar at all (and so not strictly comparable). It is largely a matter of texture. Whereas Strauss— for instance in the 'Uncle Greifenklau' section— tends to be homophonic (melody plus chordal accompaniment), in Mahler the texture is often so fragmented that it is hard to tell what 'melody' and 'accompaniment' mean. Their attitudes are symbolised in their respective

9

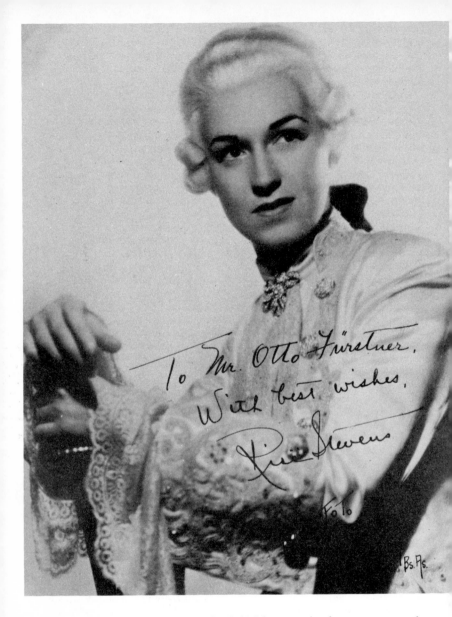

Risë Stevens as Octavian — a much admired interpretation for many years at the Metropolitan from 1938. (Covent Garden Archives)

treatments of the waltz: whereas Mahler builds it up, distorts it and makes it more complex, Strauss simplifies it, purifies it and indeed gives it back something of its pre-Mahlerian character. (This is perhaps too great a generalisation for *Rosenkavalier*, where one finds every possible kind of waltz, from the most sublimated–the Trio!–to the most vulgarised.)

So the work is not a tone poem. It is not, except for a few, rather untypical passages, music drama either–to the extent that 'music drama' is equated with late Wagner. True, it has leitmotifs, but they are nearly all melodic; there is none of the density, none of the rapid succession of textures and tone-colours, that we find in late Wagner, where 'motif' means harmony or timbre as often as it means melodic line. And the 'highlights' of the opera, its 'great moments'–the Marschallin's monologue, the Presentation of the Silver Rose, the Trio–are pure lyricism. Strauss loved the sound of the soprano voice, and here we hear it again and again–solo, *à 2* and *à 3*. Hofmannsthal, who came out with all sorts of criticisms of the work after it was complete (he made the present point in 1928), thought that 'the life of the whole thing is centred on the orchestra'. But though the orchestra often has the tune, the tune is more lyrical than is customary in Wagner, and as likely as not it will already have been heard in a vocal part. Again it is a matter of texture. The texture of *Rosenkavalier*–of its 'highlights', anyway–is closer to Mozart, or Verdi, or Tchaikovsky, than it is to Wagner; and if one looks for a passage in which the orchestra is given its head–as in the *Feuersnot* love scene, or Elektra's last waltz, or Daphne's transformation–the closest one gets is the Trio, where the voices are used as extra stops on a vast organ, everything doubling everything else. In *Rosenkavalier*, ultimately, the voice dominates.

Is it number opera, then? No, because it is still continuous. Operetta? Hardly. What *Rosenkavalier* 'is', if it can be tied down so specifically, is a hybrid of all these things: number opera for the set pieces, music drama for the transitions, operetta for quite extended sections (notably the end of Act Two and the beginning of Act Three). At some points it even breaks down into accompanied speech. Texture, pace, tone are constantly changing–sometimes with a bump, as on the third-act entry of the Marschallin–but these very changes, which make the work so hard to define, are also part of its fascination.

*

Now we have a better idea of what it is, we can look at some of the critical orthodoxies surrounding it. The most uncritical of these critical views, indeed the most banal of all banalities about Strauss, is that it constitutes a 'retreat' from the discoveries of *Salome* and *Elektra*. This view must be seen in its historical context. It originated with Schoenberg and his followers, who regarded Strauss as having deserted the modernist cause at a crucial time. It would be a distortion of Schoenberg's views to say he thought there was only one way for music to go (i.e. his way); but that is the assumption underlying the hostility to *Rosenkavalier*. If we look at *Salome* and *Elektra* more carefully, we find that the 'modernism' is largely surface, the instant response to a poetic idea. Wherever the texture is continuous–as in Salome's Dance, or the *Elektra* Recognition Scene, or the whole waltz-finale–it is as simple, and the harmony often as diatonic, as anything in *Rosenkavalier*. We think of *Salome* and *Elektra* as 'modern' works, with little islands of vocal beauty amid the chromatic turmoil. But we can also think of them (and it becomes easier to do so as the years go by) as giant puff pastries with occasional ventures into modernism. If we do, *Rosenkavalier* emerges as part of a continuous process, a process of purification which had begun long before the *Alpine*

11

Symphony. 'Purification' here means self-discovery, deciding what one can do best, freeing oneself of unwanted influences. There is a letter from Strauss to Hofmannsthal (1916) in which he writes: 'I feel downright called upon to become the Offenbach of the 20th century… Sentimentality and parody are the sensations to which my talent responds most forcefully and productively'. If we think back to the tone poems we realise this was true all along: *Don Juan*, *Don Quixote* and *Till* are the most successful. In the operatic field, *Feuersnot* (but musically it is uneven), then nothing till *Rosenkavalier*, *Ariadne*, etc.. From this point of view *Salome* and *Elektra*–and, looking ahead, even such a work as *Die Frau ohne Schatten*–appear as marvellous distractions, diversions from what Strauss was really best suited to do.

Rosenkavalier, where sentimentality and parody are of the essence, puts him back on course: for 'retreat' read 'advance'! After *Ariadne* there is the *Bourgeois Gentilhomme* music, *Arabella*, *Capriccio* and the late instrumental works. Finally come the *Four Last Songs*, in which sentimentality is 'raised to the level of great art'. The question here is not whether sentimentality and parody are worthy concerns in themselves, merely whether they were right for Strauss. Surely the works prove they were. If we take the Schoenbergian line we end up saying that everything Strauss wrote after *Elektra* constitutes a 40-year decline, followed by the inexplicable miracle of the *Four Last Songs*. This is not very helpful. If on the other hand we view his work as a continuous process of purification, a discovering of opportunities to use those particular resources with which he was so well endowed (in this context we could almost call them 'gifts'), then there is no problem. The 'simplicities' of *Rosenkavalier*– the clear textures, the diatonic harmonies, the vocal domination, the sheer *enjoyability* of the thing–these are all part of a progress to the late songs.

Rosenkavalier has, nevertheless, been abused pretty consistently over the years, though not by the general public. 'All we find… is a worn-out, dissipated *demi-mondaine*, with powdered face, rouged lips, false hair, and a hideous leer. Strauss's muse has lost her chastity' (Cecil Gray, writing in 1924). 'Strauss's most cynical, most rambling, and most repetitious work in proportion to its length' (William Austin, 1966). Times have changed, but not the tone. Here it seems more profitable to see what the two authors of the work had to say about it after its success. Hofmannsthal was always making criticisms. In a single letter of 1916 he faults Strauss's treatment of a chorus in Act Two, his music for the servants at the end of Act One, and the Baron's final exit. Twelve years later he dismisses the entire libretto ('the one engaging character, the Marschallin, disappears for an act and a half and is only dragged in with difficulty at the end; the *buffo* a garrulous and repulsive fellow; the third act most artificially tacked on to the second', etc.); and three weeks before his death he refers to the 'weakish third act'. In more positive mood, however, he recognised its 'charm', that 'special *brio*' which results from 'the concentration of colourful contrasts and incidents in each separate act'–Act Two being cited as an example. Strauss of course loved the work; but he recognised its longueurs, and made cuts when he performed it. He saw clearly that 'apart from the misunderstood waltz [it had been attacked as anachronistic], the success of *Rosenkavalier* was in the entry of the Rose Bearer, the end of Act One, and the Trio!' (letter to Hofmannsthal of 1928). Both seemed to regard the work as their most successful collaboration.

What is interesting here is that, while both men understood perfectly where the work succeeded, they were less clear about where it went wrong. Hofmannsthal's remarks still bear traces of those confusions which caused the problems in the first place. Audiences are not unduly bothered by the chorus in Act Two, and the servants in Act One are a positive delight. The Baron's

Richard Mayr who created the role of Ochs in Vienna (but not in Dresden). Strauss once told him that he imagined him all the time in the role. Mayr asked whether that was really a compliment or an insult! Ernest Newman described his performance at Covent Garden in 1924, 'His smile and whistle during Annina's reading of the letter said more than a page of words could have done'.

exit is bad, but this is the fault of the libretto as much as of the music. The third act is indeed weak (Hofmannsthal's changing conception of the Marschallin was a factor here), but is the second very much better? Hofmannsthal cites it for its 'concentration', but it can seem ramshackle. Putting all these points together one sees the emergence of a pattern: that of a strong first act (ending with a reflective monologue), a weaker second and a recovery in the third. This pattern reproduces itself in *Die Frau ohne Schatten* (*The Woman without a Shadow*), *Arabella* and *Die Liebe der Danae* (*The Love of Danae*); and since the last is not to a Hofmannsthal text one must look for the explanation in Strauss. Perhaps it is simply that, being primarily a lyrical composer, he excels in music of exposition and reflection rather than in music of development and elaboration: had he written the *Ring*, *Das Rheingold* would have been musically superior to *Die Walküre*. He has a strong sense of climax, so his endings always work; but he is not so infallible in the preparation. The low-point usually comes about halfway through Act Three, when (perhaps in compensation) the music is at its busiest: Ochs's humiliation in *Rosenkavalier*, the comings and goings in *Die Frau*. Then comes the dénouement, things settle down, and Strauss is safe.

That there are 'problems' with *Rosenkavalier* not even its most ardent admirer would doubt. Perhaps–for these are not matters that can be tested–

Alfred Roller's designs were approved by Strauss and Hofmannsthal and opera houses were for years obliged to adopt the designs if they wanted to stage the opera. The sets were seen at Covent Garden in 1936 on the visit of the Dresden State Opera Company.

the plot is too thin for a work of such length. Perhaps the busyness of the action, the large number of characters, etc., are manifestations of this thinness (Hofmannsthal's equivalent to Strauss filling the texture with notes). Or perhaps the work simply falls between too many stools: the plot calls for the lightness of operetta; 'music drama' holds up the pace; but Strauss needs the continuity of music drama for the suavity and opulence of the set pieces–themselves a bow to number opera. Of course as soon as one says all this one realises that *Rosenkavalier* is what it is, that the stylistic joltings are part of its character, indeed essential to it; that the causes of its weakness are also the causes of its fascination. The positive side of the coin is this. If *Rosenkavalier* hardly works as a whole, it is full of moments which seem to appeal to the listener in a directly personal way. It teems with memorable lines and phrases (from this point of view it is the opera-goer's *Hamlet*); and everyone has his favourite passage. It is surely this personal element–the feeling that the listener is being wooed, or cajoled, as well as being taken by force (Iris Murdoch's character sensed only the latter)–that accounts for its lasting success.

Comedy for Music

Michael Kennedy

'This is no music for me', said Kaiser Wilhelm II as he left a performance of the new opera by his court conductor Richard Strauss in Berlin. He was in the minority then and has remained in it ever since, for *Der Rosenkavalier (The Knight of the Rose* or, better, *The Rose Bearer)* was an enormous and widely publicised success on its first performance at Dresden on January 26, 1911 and has since become an indispensable part of the repertoire of every opera company which aspires to international standards. True, Vienna at first ran to form and was not too sure about it, while the waltzes upset the first Milan audience, but London took it to its heart straightaway when Beecham conducted the first British performance at Covent Garden on January 29, 1913. The reasons for its success are not hard to define. It is a good story, of young love, of lustful love and of sacrificial love; it is melodious; it is spectacular; it combines Wagnerian richness with Mozartian elegance and a *Fledermaus*–Straussian waltzing gaiety; it is witty, touching, bawdy and broadly comic; its principal characters are so real that audiences feel they know them and identify with them as well as they know and identify with Shakespearean characters or those in *The Mastersingers of Nuremberg* and *The Marriage of Figaro*; it deals with high life and low life intermixed; and, by anachronistic musical means, it nostalgically captures an era, for although ostensibly about mid-eighteenth century Vienna, it is also about the world of 1910, just before the First World War changed it for ever. As the late Sir Neville Cardus wrote so tellingly, 'imagination can hear time running out like sand during the performance of *Der Rosenkavalier* in a great opera house at the height of a season'.

This last 'social' aspect of *Der Rosenkavalier* has an important *raison d'être*: it was the last convincing operatic comedy of manners which ever could be written, the last opera of dalliance and intrigue in an aristocratic provenance, because Strauss was the last musician of any importance who worked as a court *Kapellmeister*–at Meiningen, Munich, Weimar and Berlin– and who understood the structures and traditions of that vanishing world. (He composed three autobiographies of his *Kapellmeister* life, the orchestral tone-

Richard Strauss by Schmutzer
(Mansell Collection)

poem *Ein Heldenleben*, and the operas *Der Rosenkavalier* and *Ariadne auf Naxos*). It is not surprising that Strauss should have seized upon Hofmannsthal's libretto with such enthusiasm. When Hofmannsthal first described the plot to him, Strauss exclaimed, 'We'll go ahead with this. You go straight home and send Act One as soon as you can'. At certain points, Strauss composed the music for certain dramatic situations *before* he received the libretto (he even composed a stage direction by mistake!) [1]. That tells us how vividly he saw the work in his mind. And, as will be seen, the opera's most theatrically effective *coups* were nearly all Strauss's ideas. Hofmannsthal acknowledged that the composer had taught him 'a fundamental lesson in writing dramatically for music which I shall not forget'.

Der Rosenkavalier, Strauss's Opus 59, is scored for a very large orchestra, thus: 3 flutes (3rd playing piccolo); 3 oboes (3rd playing cor anglais); 3 clarinets; bass clarinet (also basset-horn); 4 horns; 3 trumpets; 3 trombones; bass tuba; timpani, bass drum, cymbals, triangle, tambourine, glockenspiel, tenor drum, side drum, bells, castanets, celesta; 2 harps; 16 first and 16 second violins, 12 violas, 10 cellos and 8 double basses. There is also an off-stage orchestra in Act Three. Before the first performance in Dresden there were 22 orchestral rehearsals. Strauss directs the conductor to reduce the number of strings in passages 'where the audibility of the words requires it'. His whole operatic career was devoted to perfecting a technique whereby the words were audible to the listeners, whatever the size of the orchestra. He was, after all, working with librettists whose words were usually well worth hearing, particularly in the case of Hofmannsthal. The parallel with *The Marriage of Figaro* extends to the casting: three of the principal rôles are sung by three sopranos, the role of Octavian being a *travesti* rôle in the Vienna tradition (comparable to the page Cherubino in Mozart). The principal male singers are baritones or basses, with the tenor reserved for a subsidiary *buffo* part. Hofmannsthal, like Da Ponte, gives an extra twist to the sexual equivocation of the *travesti* part by making the character impersonate a woman: thus a woman dressed as a man has to dress as a woman. It is interesting to note that the *travesti* rôle in *Der Rosenkavalier* was Hofmannsthal's idea but when Strauss decided to repeat the formula in the Prologue to *Ariadne auf Naxos* and to give the rôle of the young Composer to a mezzo, Hofmannsthal was horrified. In their last collaboration, *Arabella*, the heroine's sister Zdenka passes most of the opera dressed as a boy, a deception insisted upon by her impoverished parents because they cannot afford the expense of marrying off two daughters.

Act One

The opera begins with an orchestral Introduction which tells the audience unmistakably what is happening behind the not-yet-risen curtain— that a couple are making vigorous, passionate and mutually satisfying love [2]. The priapic import of the thrusting horns can scarcely be disguised. Nor has a more sensuous 'afterglow' ever been composed for strings. But haven't we heard something very like it before? Yes; Strauss's tone-poem *Don Juan*. This Introduction opens with the *leitmotiv* [1] which represents the Rosenkavalier himself, Count Octavian Rofrano, aged 17 years and two months at this point in the early years of the reign of Empress Maria Theresa of Austria. It is scored for four horns in E, with three bassoons and pizzicato cellos and basses.

---

1. 'with discreet secrecy'
2. Illustrations on pp 37/8 show how differently from early productions this scene can now be staged.

Understandably in the circumstances, it is marked *Con moto agitato*. This is immediately followed by [2] on strings, horns and woodwind, in the alien key of E flat major, almost immediately going into the tonic key of E major by means of Strauss's favourite device of a chromatic sideslip. The point of mentioning this technicality is that the listener will respond, perhaps without knowing the musical reason why, to the abrupt differentiation of character. [2] is the first of several themes to be associated with the Marschallin, or to give her her full title Die Feldmarschallin Fürstin Werdenberg (the wife of the Field Marshal Prince von Werdenberg). Now—and we are only in the fifth bar—comes another Octavian theme, [3], and, three bars later, yet another, [4], which is marked not only *agitato* but 'very extravagant in execution' (*sehr überschwerglich im Vortrag*). As the excitement grows, with trills for flutes, the D clarinet and two bassoons, Strauss directs that 'from this point the mounting excitement is to have a suggestion of parody', rather as if he were suggesting that we must not take this love affair too seriously. He underlines this point by musical parody of the love duet from Wagner's *Tristan und Isolde*. No couple can sustain such physical ecstasy for long and as the orchestral texture is thinned, the passion drains from the strings and the tempo slackens as the oboe sings out [5], clarinets, solo viola and solo cello have a touching little subsidiary figure marked 'sighing' (*seufzend*). Theme [5] is often labelled as the *leitmotiv* of 'Love's resignation' or 'Renunciation', but Strauss uses it whenever the Marschallin muses on the passing of her youth and the concomitant loss of a young lover like Octavian. The Introduction ends with a *tranquillo* coda for strings, woodwind and four horns based on the unforgettably tender melody [6] associated with the Marschallin, whom we see in bed with Octavian kneeling beside her as the curtain rises. The cellos' *molto espressivo* version of [1], now tender where it was impetuous, merges into arabesques of birdsong on woodwind. As Octavian sings his praise of his lover—' *Wie du warst! Wie du bist!* ', *lit*. 'How you were, how you are'—oboe and viola echo his sentiments with [7]. We learn that Octavian's nickname is Quinquin— (Hofmannsthal had discovered that this sobriquet belonged to Count Esterházy von Galantha, who was born in 1715, a little before Octavian). The couple continue their verbal love-making, while Strauss reduces the scoring to chamber-orchestra proportions. When Octavian becomes metaphysical about the meaning of ' you and I', cellos, later joined by violas, quietly hint at the *Tristan* love-motif. When the Marschallin declares her love, [6] floods back. The birdsong is heard again and Octavian runs to the window to draw the curtains across: if he can shut out the day, he says, he can shut out all the other people in the Marschallin's life. An *allegro* [8] begins softly on violins and woodwind and a little bell (triangle) is heard coming nearer. Octavian resents this intrusion. ' No one shall enter, I am master here', he declares, a solo horn quoting, surely ironically, the ardent theme [1] which we first heard from four horns. At whom is this defiance aimed? Only at the Marschallin's little black servant Mahomet, who is bringing her morning chocolate. It is the silver bells sewn to his tunic which we have heard as he approaches. He enters to an enchanting march [9], with a delicate orchestration including tambourine and glockenspiel. The Marschallin—who has been in this situation before—tells Octavian to hide both himself and his sword. When the page has gone she ticks off Octavian for having left his sword in view—hasn't he better manners? He resents this and [1] can be heard in a rather sulky version as he remonstrates with her. But this cloud is dispersed while they have breakfast in waltz tempo [10]. Strauss's scoring for this scene is a pretty example of period pastiche and also a reminder of his early and effective works for wind instruments (the *Serenade and Suite*). Tenderness returns, Octavian using the Marschallin's name, Marie Theres', and her pet-name, Bichette, while [4] on the strings accompanies their endearments.

The idyll is broken when Octavian remarks how lucky he is to be with her while the Field Marshal is bear-hunting in the Croatian forest. The Marschallin replies that she dreamt of her husband last night. Octavian's pride is ruffled. 'My dreams are not mine to command,' the Marschallin answers. She had dreamed of hearing the noise of his horses in the courtyard— 'and you were here!' It has reminded her of an occasion when he really had returned unexpectedly. 'For once', ('*Einmal*'), she begins, but goes no further. This infuriates Octavian, who demands in vain to know more. All this episode is scored like a scherzo, with rapid ascending flourishes for woodwind and strings as Octavian's temper flares. But now there truly is a disturbance in her dressing-room and the Marschallin is convinced it is her husband arguing with her loyal servants. She tells Octavian to hide. Beneath the agitated strings which tell of her anxiety, an ungainly theme is heard on the bass tuba. As the voice in the anteroom grows louder, she goes to the door to listen. 'That is not my husband's voice', she cries. 'They're saying Herr Baron to him'. And as she calls 'Quinquin, it's someone else', the music, sharing her relief, goes into waltz-time. She identifies 'that stupid loutish voice' as belonging to her cousin Baron Ochs from Lerchenau. Then she remembers that a few days ago (when she was out with Octavian) she was handed a letter. 'That was a letter from Ochs and I've no idea what was in it.' Octavian's [1] is transformed into the waltz theme [11] on oboes and flutes as he re-appears dressed as a chambermaid in skirt and short jacket with his hair tied in a handkerchief and ribbon for a cap. 'She' addresses the Marschallin in broad Viennese dialect ('Y'know I've not been long in Your Highness' household here') and the Marschallin responds delightedly, 'You dear. And only one kiss may I give you. That's for your wages.' ('*Du, Schatz! Und nicht einmal mehr als ein Busserl kann ich Dir geben*'.) All this to a lilting waltz, the musical embodiment of a light-hearted masquerade. Every bar of the score up to this point is indicative of Strauss's delight when he received the Act One libretto: 'It'll set itself to music like oil and melted butter: I'm hatching it out already'[3]. He scarcely needed Hofmannsthal's injunction 'Do try and think of an old-fashioned Viennese waltz, sweet and yet saucy, which must pervade the whole of the last act'[4]; waltzes were to pervade the whole score. Censorious English critics in the 1930s rapped Strauss over the knuckles because they thought that his anachronistic use of waltzes was characteristic of his 'carelessness in the matter of style'! Both he and Hofmannsthal by giving Vienna the waltz eighty years early also gave opera a masterstroke of imaginative genius in the creation of an atmosphere.

Baron Ochs (baritone) bursts into the room to a loud diminished seventh chord scored for brass, woodwind and strings. Now the music becomes *langsam und gravitätisch* (slow and weighty). He has bumped into Octavian-in-disguise and, ignoring the Marschallin, shows his immediate interest in this 'pretty child' ('*hübsches Kind*'). It is important to know how Strauss visualised this great character. He wrote in an essay on *Der Rosenkavalier* in 1942[5]: 'Ochs must be a rustic Don Juan beau of about thirty-five, always a nobleman (even if a rather boorish one), who knows how to conduct himself decently in the Marschallin's salon, so that she does not have him thrown out by her servants after five minutes. He is a bounder *inwardly*; but on the

3. Letter to Hofmannsthal, April 21, 1909.
4. Letter to Strauss, April 24, 1909.
5   R. Strauss: *Recollections and Reflections*, Zürich 1949, London 1953.

Kurt Böhme as Ochs at Covent Garden, 1959. (Covent Garden Archives)

surface sufficiently presentable . . . Ochs's first scene in the bedroom must be played with the utmost delicacy and discretion . . . . In other words: Viennese comedy not Berlin farce'. All this is summarised in the theme [12] to which he makes his ungainly obeisance–the French bow–to the Marschallin. He is at ease with her, reminding her that he has even called on another princess while that particular lady was having a bath.

In the scene that follows Ochs–in the easy *parlando* recitative style which Strauss began to develop in *Feuersnot* (1900–1) and *Salome* (1904–5), perfected here and in *Ariadne auf Naxos* (1912–16) and used with supreme brilliance in *Intermezzo* (1917–23), *The Silent Woman* (1933–4) and *Capriccio* (1940–1)–is torn between making passes at Octavian and explaining his mission to the Marschallin. For her part, the Marschallin is trying to signal to Octavian to leave and at the same time to make sense of Ochs's narrative (he, naturally, assumes she has read his letter; she has to equivocate). The scoring continues airy and allusive with much use of [13]–a lifetime of acquaintance with the opera will still reveal new subtleties in Strauss's web of motifs. Ochs has come to consult his cousin about his forthcoming marriage to Sophie von Faninal–at the first mention of her a solo cello plays a theme later to be associated with her [14]. She is, he says, fresh from a convent, a mere puppy, healthy, well-washed ('*Pudeljung! Gesund! Gewaschen!*'), only child of the newly ennobled Faninal who has made a pile of money by supplying the army in the Netherlands. He makes no secret that the money is the principal attraction. While Octavian, whom the Marschallin now addresses as Mariandel, serves Ochs with some of the breakfast chocolate, the Baron asks the favour he has come about. Hofmannsthal invented a Viennese custom by which a silver rose had to be presented to a bride-to-be on behalf of an aristocratic bridegroom by a nobly-born ambassador; Ochs asks her to recommend someone for this task. The Marschallin suggests he should dine with her next day and she will propose a name. But Ochs is not to be dismissed so easily: he also requests the services of her lawyer. The Marschallin sees another chance of getting Octavian out of the room and, as the music goes back into waltz tempo, orders 'her' to see if the lawyer is awaiting her morning levée. A new theme [15] is heard when Ochs refers to Mariandel as 'such a treasure' ('*ein solches Goldkind*') and stops 'her' exit. At this point the Major-Domo enters to report the arrival of 'the customary riff-raff' for the levée. Meanwhile Ochs is trying to 'date' Mariandel for a supper *tête-à-tête* and when she says 'I don't really know if I ought' ('*I weiss halt nit, ob i dös derf*') bassoons play a waltz theme to be closely associated with Ochs [16]. When the Marschallin laughingly taunts Ochs for flirting even though he is engaged, he launches into a scherzo-like monologue [17] describing how men do not mate by the calendar like animals: there is not a season nor an hour of the day when he is not ready to seduce a woman.

Strauss had reached this point when he told Hofmannsthal[6]: 'My work is flowing along like the Loisach: I am composing everything–neck and crop. I am starting on the levée tomorrow'. This he had already described as 'not easy to put into shape, but I'll manage it all right... I'll need very good actors again; the ordinary operatic singers won't do'. He had written the Baron's scene but wanted more lines for it, as well as words for 'a great musical conclusion in the form of a trio... I want him to go on bragging of all the things he can do, piling it on thicker and thicker, preferably in a dactylic rhythm... overlaid by a duet of the Marschallin, continuing along the theme of "You are going too far! Leave the child alone".... And on top of it Octavian, whom I want to let burst into loud laughter.... Would you add some more text here: the music is all ready and I only need the words for accompaniment and filling in'.[7] This illustrates Strauss's earlier statement that 'for the sake of symphonic unity I must compose the music from the beginning to the end'.

When this trio ends, Ochs asks if he can have Mariandel as servant for his

6. Letter to Hofmannsthal, May 16, 1909.
7. Letter to Hofmannsthal, May 16, 1909.

Elizabeth Schwarzkopf (the Marschallin) suggests that the miniature portrait of Octavian is worth Ochs's attention, in Robin Ironside's designs, with Sena Jurinacs as Octavian and Kurt Böhme as Ochs; Covent Garden, 1959. (Covent Garden Archives)

bride–'she' seems to have 'a drop of good blood' and could be 'a young princess'. He then reveals that his own bastard son acts as his body-servant and will deliver the silver rose to the Marschallin. The Marschallin picks up this clue to explain away Mariandel as Octavian's bastard sister (she realises Ochs is bound to meet Octavian sooner or later) and shows Ochs a medallion of Octavian, suggesting him as the Rose-Bearer. Ochs immediately sees the resemblance to the maid. This dialogue, from Ochs's 'Gad, should be a young princess' ('*Könnt' eine junge Fürstin sein*'), is accompanied by a languid version of the waltz [15] which represents Octavian as Mariandel and, in this wistful setting, perhaps implies that the Marschallin senses danger in employing Octavian as Rose-Bearer. She now orders Mariandel to let in the waiting throng, and the maid escapes at last, slamming the door in Ochs's face.

The levée, based on 'The Contessa's Morning Levée', the fourth engraving in Hogarth's series *Marriage à la Mode*, is one of Strauss's big set-pieces in which his gift for character-vignettes, familiar from the tone-poems *Till Eulenspiegel*, *Ein Heldenleben* and *Don Quixote*, enables him to present a busy, colourful scene. On to the stage now come footmen, a lawyer, a chef, a kitchen-boy with menu-book, a milliner, a scholar, an animal-vendor with dogs and monkey, a singer and flautist, a soldier's widow with her three

21

children, and two intriguers, Valzacchi (tenor) and his niece Annina (contralto). The three orphaned children implore protection to a lugubrious chant which is interrupted by the various salesmen's cries (the animal-vendor's cry is a quotation from the baby's yells in his bath in the *Symphonia Domestica*, a Garmisch 'in-joke', since the vendor is singing about monkeys and housetrained puppies). The Marschallin introduces her lawyer to Ochs, and Valzacchi, accompanied by a rapid conspiratorial theme [18] on bass clarinet and muted cellos, tries to interest her in a scandal-sheet. She gives the grateful orphans money and a kiss and her hairdresser attends to her coiffure. This scene now becomes a stylised period-piece in minuet tempo, with an elaborate flute part which serves both to illustrate the hairdresser's flying fingers and to introduce the Tenor's *Di rigori armato il seno* [19], Strauss's testing but affectionate parody of an Italian operatic aria (purloined by Hofmannsthal from the petit-ballet in the fifth act of Molière's *Le bourgeois gentilhomme*).

Ochs has now been joined by his three uncouth servants, one of them his illegitimate son Leopold ('a tall young fellow with a foolish, insolent expression'). He is propounding to the astonished lawyer that his marriage settlement (*Morgengrabe*), instead of being from him to his bride, shall be from her to him and shall consist of his own family estates free of all mortgages. A new theme [20] is signalled by various instruments before it is heard in full on strings and horns. The Tenor begins his second stanza accompanied not only by the flute but by the argument of Ochs and the lawyer. Ochs bangs the table angrily, the Tenor is cut off in mid-aria, and the Marschallin complains that the hairdresser has made her look old. The hairdresser works feverishly to change the style (agitated flutes again) and the Marschallin signs that the levée is ended. While the stage empties, Valzacchi and Annina offer their services to Ochs in a quicksilver *prestissimo* piece of scoring based on [21] and he mentions Mariandel to them. Ochs, to a reprise of [12], introduces Leopold to the Marschallin. The youth gives her the case containing the silver rose. To the music of Sophie's theme [14] and her own love-theme [6], she assures Ochs that Octavian will act as Rose-bearer.

Now the mood and tenor of the opera change. The Marschallin is left alone for the first time. The wonderful coda contains three superb arias for this woman who, though she appears in only half the opera, dominates it. Although the music he wrote for her in the Introduction shows that Strauss realised her importance from the start, Hofmannsthal did not (like Wagner with Hans Sachs) fully realise it until the libretto was far advanced. Then he wrote[8]: 'She is the central figure for the public, for the women above all, the figure with whom they feel and *move*'. It is important, again, to know how Strauss visualised her–'a young and beautiful woman of not more than 32 who, when she is in a bad mood, occasionally feels herself an "old hag" compared with 17-year-old Octavian'. In the 18th century 32 was older than it is today, but the practice of making the Marschallin a woman in her fifties is a distortion of the composer's intentions.

Ochs's [12] is now transformed into something like a tragic theme by violins and violas over a plodding bass as the Marschallin muses on the Baron's attitude to his marriage. The orchestral texture is reduced to that of a chamber orchestra as solo strings and clarinet introduce [22], a theme very similar to the opening of *Till Eulenspiegel*, when she remembers how she herself had come from a convent to an arranged marriage. She looks in her mirror, contemplates her old age and how the crowds will point her out as the old

8.   Letter to Strauss, June 6, 1910.

Adele Leigh as Octavian in riding costume. (Covent Garden Archives)

Princess. The oboe poignantly quotes [5] as she reflects that this all has to be endured–the difference lies in *how* ('*Wie*') one endures it. And on the word '*Wie*' a bare octave on the harp gives a sharp pang to the strings' gentle chord. Octavian re-enters in riding kit. He senses the Marschallin's changed mood and tries to cheer her up and to protest his love to an orchestral background compounded of their love themes and their earlier discussion of the Field Marshal. She gently rejects Octavian's advances and reflects that nothing will last, that even he will desert her. Now, in a tranquil 6/8, she begins her monologue on the strangeness of time [23], how one is suddenly aware of it, how she sometimes gets up in the night to stop all the clocks (and their soft chimes are magically evoked by celesta and two harps playing harmonics), how her belief in God comforts her. Octavian's response, sensuously tender, is to offer himself as a more accessible substitute for God, but the Marschallin insists that one day he will leave her for a younger and more beautiful woman– and she sings those words, prophetically, to a variation of Sophie's [14]. They argue heatedly but the Marschallin insists it will happen, today or tomorrow

23

('*Heut' oder Morgen*'), and asks Octavian to leave. In her third and most touching solo, which is the quintessence of nostalgia, based on the themes [5] and [2] and with melting *glissandi* in the strings, she describes how she will go to church, visit her old and ailing uncle Greifenklau (*lit.* Griffon-claw) and ride in the Prater where Octavian, if he wishes, may join her. Moved, Octavian leaves. (Strauss knew he had done well here: 'that certain Viennese sentimentality of the parting scene has come off very well. My wife likes it very much', he told his librettist[9].) The orchestra bursts out as the Marschallin panics–she has not even kissed him. She sends her footmen after him but they breathlessly report that they have missed him. In the nostalgic key of E flat, she calls for Mahomet, [9a], and, to the expressive music of [6], orders him to take the silver rose to Octavian. The act ends with her deep in thought as the solo violin and high woodwind play a transfigured version of Octavian's principal motif [1].

Act Two

This act, set in Faninal's palatial home, gave the collaborators much more trouble than Act One. The published Correspondence reveals the fascinating changes which were made. Suffice it to say that Strauss received the libretto to Act Two in June 1909. On July 9 he wrote the first of several detailed criticisms. It lacked 'the necessary clash and climax ... if Act Two falls flat the opera is lost'. He accepted it up to Ochs's entrance. Thereafter everything that happens was Strauss's idea, including such details as Ochs's neglecting to

9. Letter to Hofmannsthal, May 22, 1909.

Elizabeth Schumann as Sophie, who created the role in Hamburg a few weeks after the Dresden premiere in 1911, and continued to sing it through-out her career (many times opposite Lehmann at Covent Garden) until 1938.

Tiana Lemnitz as Octavian, 1936. (Covent Garden Archives)

tip Annina at the end, and he asked Hofmannsthal for 'much more witty and polished' dialogue, adding: 'Don't forget that the audience should also laugh! *Laugh*, not just smile or grin!' Hofmannsthal was not offended. 'I realise myself that for the stage the new version is very much more effective . . . and I am very grateful for your energetic intervention.'

The prelude illustrates, *molto allegro*, the excitement of the preparations for the arrival of the Rose-Bearer [24, 25]. An imposing version of the wedding theme [20] is heard in canon and the prelude ends with [25] followed by a richly scored fanfare for his ambassador [26]. Faninal (baritone) hails this great and holy day and leaves Sophie with her duenna, Marianne Leitmetzerin (soprano). While the duenna reports everything that is happening in the street, Sophie sings [27] of her lonely state, motherless in this solemn hour. But Marianne's description of the Rose-Bearer's procession, the couriers' off-stage calls of Rofrano and the orchestra's recollection of [1] and [26] bring her to an agitated pitch of anticipation. To an emphatic *fortissimo* [26] followed by a fully-scored chord of F sharp major, with a cymbal-clash and rolls of drums and triangle, the doors open to reveal Octavian, a dazzling figure in silver from head to foot and holding out the silver rose. The justly famous and beloved Presentation of the Silver Rose is based on [28] (derived from Sophie's [14]), first heard on the oboe and marked 'very expressively' (*sehr ausdrucksvoll*), with the addition of the unforgettable glittering [28b], scored for 3 flutes, 3 solo violins, celesta and two harps, which is repeated several times throughout the presentation. Octavian diffidently offers the rose. Sophie accepts it, remarks on its scent (from a drop of Persian attar) and, in a soaring ecstatic phrase, describes it as 'like heavenly, not earthly flowers' ('*Wie himmlische, nicht irdische, wie Rosen*'). For the first time their eyes meet and, very softly, a solo trumpet plays [29], the theme of love-at-first-sight to which they later sing their rapturous duet. Strauss then subtly relaxes

Valerie Masterson (Sophie) and Josephine Barstow (Octavian) in the ENO production by John Copley.

the tension into a slightly formal, almost embarrassed conversation (*animato grazioso*) between the two young people, supervised by the duenna. Sophie tells Octavian she knows his age and all his names [30], and she even knows that his close friends call him Quinquin. It is another of those moments of repose in which the opera abounds.

But now Ochs and his disreputable retinue are introduced by Faninal, to a march-like version of [25]. Ochs inspects Sophie as if she were horse-flesh, to Octavian's fury and Sophie's disgust. He remarks on Octavian's likeness to 'a certain someone' and reveals the existence of 'a little bastard sister', before he tries to woo Sophie on his knee. Faninal is complacently delighted by what he sees, Octavian enraged. Ochs continues to tease Sophie, who asks 'What are you to me?'. Ochs's obvious reply–that she will discover the answer overnight–leads him to quote his favourite song and the line (*lit.*) 'with me no night will be too long' ('*Mit mir keine Nacht dir zu lang*'). This is the most famous tune in the opera [31, 32]. It was written as a parody of Johann Strauss but has equalled the real thing in the public's affections. (Undoubtedly this is some of the music Strauss wrote in advance of the libretto, since tune and words do not fit each other all that well.) Ochs, revelling in what he calls 'the luck of the Lerchenaus' [33], is then taken by Faninal to attend to legal formalities, but before he goes he invites Octavian to take what liberties he likes with the 'young unbroken filly'.

Left together (except for the duenna) Sophie appeals for Octavian's help [34]. There is a sudden uproar as Ochs's men chase Faninal's maids through the room, and the duenna leaves to aid the Major-Domo. Now the lovers are alone. They enjoy their first kiss and their duet [35] is a tender affair, Strauss having obeyed Hofmannsthal's injunction to avoid 'a Wagnerian kind of erotic screaming'. On its last note Valzacchi and Annina, who have tiptoed in, seize them and call for Ochs. Octavian decides, rather ineffectually, to tell the Baron of Sophie's dislike but Ochs contemptuously mocks him. When the Baron tries to steer Sophie into the room where the lawyer is waiting, Octavian bars their way, flings insults at the Baron and draws his sword. Ochs summons his followers with a piercing whistle, but the sight of the sword deters them. In a scuffle Ochs brushes its point and yells 'Murder'. A farcical ensemble (all Strauss's idea) follows, in which Ochs is tended, most incompetently, by his retinue and a doctor; Faninal's servants fill the stage wondering what has happened, while Annina harangues them, saying that Octavian and Sophie were already secretly engaged; the duenna helps to tend Ochs; and Faninal toadies to Ochs (and, feeling very sorry for himself, rounds on his daughter, telling her she has the choice of marriage to Ochs's corpse if necessary or a convent for life). Sophie is now all defiance, and Octavian leaves with a whispered word to Valzacchi and Annina.

Faninal's posturings irritate Ochs, who asks for some wine in order to get rid of him. This ensemble is a masterly example of Strauss's ability to keep the top spinning while the stage action is predominant. Ochs, his arm now in a sling, bemoans his fate in Vienna and curses Octavian who has caused his arm to hurt when he tries to drink. (His monologue was inspired by Falstaff's '*Mondo ladro*' in Verdi's opera when the Fat Knight has climbed dripping from the Thames and warms himself with wine.) A gentler version of [12], however, tells us that Ochs is feeling better and the 'luck of the Lerchenaus' theme [33] (and other waltzes [31]) accompanies his amusement at the memory of Sophie's tantrums. Annina now comes in with a letter, which Ochs asks her to read aloud. It is from Mariandel–now we know what Octavian was saying to the conspirators before he left–suggesting a meeting next evening and awaiting an answer. Ochs is overjoyed. Ignoring Annina's importuning for a tip, he tells her to set up a writing-table and he will dictate his reply. The orchestra plays a sumptuous version of [31] and Ochs contentedly sings the last lines, ending on a low E held for six bars. (Some basses improve on the score and go down to C and who can blame them!) Strauss wrote to Hofmannsthal on September 18, 1909: 'The final conclusion of Act Two is now all composed and, I believe, has turned out a first-class hit. "I am satisfied with myself"'.

Act Three

Hofmannsthal wrote to Strauss on September 20, 1909: 'As soon as I have got my comedy out of the way, I shall tackle Act Three.... It must become the best of all, gay and full of feeling, and ought, in the character of the Marschallin, to touch once again the more sublime chords of tenderness'. Some time early in 1910 the libretto of the first part of the act reached Strauss. But he wanted it all. On April 23 he wrote, 'I am in Garmisch and am in agonies waiting for Act Three!'; Hofmannsthal's reply four days later promised more but added: 'Only the very end, the trio-duet, which needs much subtlety and yet great sweetness, has had to be put off until now when I am feeling better and more in the mood.... I did so want to write this last scene, a matter of only three or four pages, out in the garden'. By May 2, Strauss had started to compose Act Three. It is interesting to know that as early as June 26, 1909, Strauss told his librettist that 'for the end of Act Three, the softly-fading duet of Sophie and Octavian, I have a very pretty tune'. He then asked for 12 to 16 lines in a particular rhythm. Nearly a year later, when Hofmannsthal came to write the words of the duet, he told Strauss he was 'obviously very much tied down by the metre scheme which you presented for me, but in the end I found it rather agreeable to be bound in this way to a given tune since I felt in this something Mozartian...'. At this stage the intention was still to call the opera *Ochs von Lerchenau*. Not until June 10, 1910 did the title *Rosenkavalier* occur in the correspondence. One further quotation illustrates the delight and care with which this masterpiece was created. Hofmannsthal to Strauss, May 4, 1910: 'I would have found the end long ago but for the appalling weather..... The end must be *very* good, or it will be no good at all. It must be psychologically convincing and at the same time tender, the words must be charming and easy to sing, it must be properly split up into conversation and again into numbers, it must provide a happy ending for the young people and yet not make one too uncomfortable about the Marschallin. In short, it must be done with zest and joy, and so I must sit in the garden and have sun, not icy rainstorms'.

The third act opens with a long orchestral Introduction and Pantomime, *vivace possibile*. It is a fugato based on the conspirators' themes [18] and [21] and their derivatives, and it obviously describes conspiratorial activities. Octavian's [1] is presented in mercurial shape, Ochs's [25] mockingly. The scoring is light-fingered. When the first bars are repeated, the curtain rises on a private room in an inn in a disreputable suburb of Vienna. Annina is disguised in mourning and Valzacchi is adjusting her veil. Octavian, in his Mariandel disguise but wearing riding boots beneath his skirt, makes a brief appearance. He throws a purse to Valzacchi. Valzacchi shows five men to hiding-places under trap-doors, and behind fake windows and sliding panels. He claps his hands and they rehearse their 'materialisations' and 'disappearances' [36]. A waiter and a boy light candles (woodwind trills) and arrange the dining-table. So far not a word has been sung, while the orchestra has played a string of waltzes. We hear much of Ochs's [16] and of Octavian-as-Mariandel's [11]. As the candles are lit, an off-stage orchestra begins to play more waltzes, one of which is [16], but the others–[37], [38], associated with the waiters, and [39]–are new[10]. Strauss here shows himself the equal of Johann Strauss in *Die Fledermaus*. Indeed, he himself wrote in 1925: 'How could I have written the *Rosenkavalier* waltzes without the example of the merry genius of Vienna?'.

Ochs, his arm still in a sling, enters with Mariandel. He extinguishes the candles, complains about the music, and says he does not need the waiters, because his Leopold will serve the meal. Alone with Mariandel at last, he pours some wine for her, which she refuses to the languid strain of [40]. She says she wants to leave and 'mistaking' a curtained alcove for an exit, discloses a bed. 'Who's it for?' 'You'll know in good time', Ochs replies[11]. As he pulls Mariandel towards him, her resemblance to 'that blasted boy' disturbs him, and an eruption in the brass disturbs the flow of waltzes [41, 42]. One of the trap-door apparitions [36] jumps the gun and terrifies Ochs. Mariandel (who has signalled to the man to close his door) pacifies the Baron. The off-stage band now strikes up with [31] in a highly schmaltzy version, which to Ochs's ill-concealed irritation, reduces Mariandel to maudlin tears [43]. He removes his wig, revealing a bald scalp, and grapples with Mariandel's bodice. This prompts Octavian to signal for pandemonium to break loose on stage and in the orchestra. The apparitions appear, one of them takes the wig, while another–the disguised Annina–threatens Ochs and then claims histrionically that he is her husband. Children dance round him screaming 'Papa!'. Ochs opens the window and calls for the police. The Police Commissar (bass baritone) questions Ochs and the landlord. Although Ochs says Valzacchi will vouch for him, the Italian, firmly in Octavian's pay, knows nothing, of course. Leopold, concerned at the way things are going, runs out. He has gone, as we shall discover, to fetch the Marschallin–this was Strauss's explanation for the arrival of this high-born lady in such an unlikely place. Yes, it is a creaky part of the plot but, by now, who cares? At the moment Ochs tells the Commissar that Mariandel is his fiancée, Sophie von Faninal, in walks Faninal (summoned by Valzacchi on Octavian's instructions, but thinking he has been called by Ochs). Ochs tries to disown Faninal. The orchestra is a web of thematic fragments which sustain the mood during the tomfoolery. Strauss found this part of the plot 'rather heavy going for a musician', and sometimes it sounds it.

When the Commissar asks Faninal if Mariandel is his daughter, as Ochs has said, Faninal sends for Sophie, who is sitting outside in the sedan. Her entry restores some dignity to the scene and begins the stretch of magnificent music with which Strauss achieved the opera's emotional crisis. A splendid new version for full orchestra of one of her themes announces her arrival [44], accompanied (when they are not cut, as they often are) by a chorus of onlookers muttering 'The bride–oh what a sore disgrace!'. Faninal indicates Annina and the children to her as Ochs's wife and children and then collapses. She helps him to an anteroom. Meanwhile, Ochs has found his wig and begins to feel more like his old self. He tells the Commissar that he'll pay the bill and

---

10. The instrumentation of the off-stage band is: 2 flutes, oboe, 1 clarinet in C, 2 clarinets in B, 2 bassoons, 2 horns, 1 trumpet, 1 side-drum, 1 harmonium, 1 piano, violins, violas, cellos, double-basses.
11. In the original 1913 English translation by Alfred Kalisch, there was no mention of the bed. This opera fell foul of the censors in Berlin in 1911, when many lines (especially in Ochs's Act One monologue) were bowdlerised, and until quite recently the Marschallin was never seen in bed on stage.

drive Mariandel home; but the Commissar has more questions for him. The music stops and Octavian asks to make a statement where Ochs cannot hear him. He retires to the alcove, and, as Ochs assures the constables that he has no idea who Annina is, Octavian tosses Mariandel's undergarments to the Commissar (to a 6/8 version of [43]). The excitement mounts until the landlord announces the arrival of the Marschallin.

This great theatrical moment is the fulcrum of the plot, as Hofmannsthal intended it to be. Strauss wrote to him[12]: 'The Marschallin's entrance and the ensuing scene must be the focal point of the action and the suspense, and must be highly concentrated. When the Baron and the whole crowd are gone, then everything can gradually dissolve into a lyrical mood and return to soft outlines'. Hofmannsthal wrote[13] interestingly about his characters' personalities: 'Sophie is a very pretty girl, but she is also a very ordinary girl like dozens of others–this is the whole point of the story; true charm of speech, indeed the stronger charm of personality is all with the Marschallin. Just the fact that, in this criss-cross double adventure, Quinquin falls for the *very first* little girl to turn up, that is the point, that is what unites the whole and holds together the two actions. The Marschallin remains the dominant female figure, between Ochs and Quinquin–Sophie always stands one step below these chief characters . . . . Even the musical, conceptual unity of the whole opera would suffer if the personality of the Marschallin were to be deprived of her full stature...'. Strauss scarcely needed this lesson in the creation of operatic women. Already in *Salome* and *Elektra*, he had shown his insight into feminine psychology, and after *Der Rosenkavalier* he was to add further portraits to this gallery, Zerbinetta and Ariadne in *Ariadne auf Naxos*, the Empress and the Dyer's Wife in *Die Frau ohne Schatten*, his own wife Pauline in *Intermezzo*, the charming Arabella, the humanised mythological characters Helen, Daphne and Danae, and (nearest of all to the Marschallin) the Countess in his wonderful last opera *Capriccio*. Many would argue that the Marschallin remains his greatest creation. He certainly was in no doubt how to project her in the closing pages of the opera. As late as September 10, 1910

12. Letter to Hofmannsthal, May 20, 1910.
13. Letter to Strauss, July 12, 1910.

*Viorica Ursuleac as the Marschallin
(Covent Garden Archives)*

Hofmannsthal had misgivings about the ending and sent Strauss a shortened version. Strauss's reply was to the point: 'That it sounds a bit flat in reading is obvious. But it is at the conclusion that a musician, if he has any ideas at all, can achieve his best and supreme effects–so you may safely leave this for me to judge'. How right he was can now be heard.

The Marschallin is followed by little Mahomet carrying her train. A sumptuous and stately version of [5] is played on high woodwind and high strings–one can almost hear the sweep of her dress–and on the basset-horn, bassoons and cellos is a quickened version of [1] as Octavian puts his head between the curtains of the alcove to ask what brings her here. The Marschallin ignores him while she recognises the Commissar as having been her husband's orderly. Ochs, who signals to Leopold his pleasure at the success of his 'rescue' mission, is convinced the Marschallin has come to extricate him and gestures to Octavian (still Mariandel to him) to stay in the alcove, but when he turns his back Octavian, now in male attire, steps out. Sophie returns, does not see the Marschallin, and tells Ochs she has a message from Faninal. That, says Octavian to the Marschallin, is the girl for whose sake... he needs to say no more. 'Who she is I can surely guess. She has great charm,' the Marschallin replies icily, for the only time in the opera addressing Octavian as Rofrano. (Among the delights of Hofmannsthal's libretto are the subtleties of language and etiquette, some of them lost in translation, and the use of dialect for Ochs and Mariandel.) Sophie shows herself something of a spitfire, telling Ochs that Faninal warns him not to come within a hundred paces of his house, or else. She here adopts the aristocratic third-person style of address. Theme [24], Faninal's principal motif, crackles through the orchestra during this outburst.

When Ochs tries to push past Sophie into the room where Faninal is resting, the Marschallin orders him to put a good face on the situation and to leave with dignity. Parts of [12] and [13] are heard on violins, violas and woodwind as Ochs shows stupefaction. It has all been a farce, you see, the Marschallin tells the Commissar, a phrase which is echoed emptily by the shocked Sophie. To the throb of horns and basses, the Marschallin tells Octavian to make Ochs see sense. Octavian's relish in this–[1] and [16]–is obvious. When the Marschallin incautiously interjects that she is displeased with men in general at the moment [5], Ochs at last weighs up the situation between Octavian and the Marschallin and, as the tender love-theme [6] returns in splendour, says he does not know what he ought to think. 'You will just refrain from thinking', is the Marschallin's edict. Many Ochs themes recur as he believes he has triumphed over the Marschallin. He will forget everything and make it up with Faninal. With [20], the theme of the wedding preparations, in full sail in the orchestra, the Marschallin imperiously informs him that everything– including his engagement–is finished. At last, to a falling cadence similar to that in *Till Eulenspiegel* which marks the end of the rogue's escapades, Ochs faces reality. So does Sophie, who believes her love for Octavian must be finished too, and she repeats the Marschallin's *'Ist halt vorbei'* (*lit.* 'Is simply finished') to a pathetic reminiscence of the rapturous phrase with which she had received the silver rose. The Marschallin, whose thoughts are precisely similar where Octavian is concerned, sings her phrase to [5]. These musings merge into the orchestra's quiet recapitulation of the act's Introduction. To its ghostly flickering, all the conspirators enter, the landlord presenting the bill, the children screaming 'Papa'. They advance on Ochs, who calls out ' *Leupold, wir gehn!*' ('We go'). At this the waltzes return, first [33] as Annina and Valzacchi taunt him with 'the luck of the Lerchenaus' theme [31], the dinner waltz [37] and, on horns, the theme with which in Act One the

Marschallin expressed her relief that her husband had not returned. Against this kaleidoscope of sound [41], the bills are presented, the children yell, and Ochs and Leopold finally escape, chased by the crowd.

The waltz tempo of [41] continues when the Marschallin, Octavian and Sophie are left together. The masquerade really is over, and the listener will sense Strauss rising to the challenge of a deeper theme. Octavian does not know which woman to console but the Marschallin, taut and controlled, sends him to Sophie. To a simple waltz [45], Octavian asks Sophie for a tender greeting. The Marschallin's renunciation theme [5] is merged into [45]; and there is another reminiscence from Act One as she recalls her words ' *Heut' oder Morgen*' ('Today or tomorrow') while she watches Octavian reiterate his love to Sophie. In this ensemble, [45] combines with the Act One love-duet in a passionate climax. It is Sophie now who is perceptive, and sends Octavian to the distressed Marschallin, saying she must go to her father. When Octavian orders her to stay, the Marschallin approaches Sophie and, with [5] *con moto grazioso* on the first violins, asks if she already loves Octavian so much. The embarrassed girl, turning into a nervous chatterbox, ascribes her pale cheeks to the shock she has had over her father. The Marschallin, worldly-wise and kindly, stops her prattle. She knows the cure for Faninal's ills; she will invite him to drive home with her in her carriage, along with Sophie herself and Octavian.

The young lovers are deeply moved. The Trio that follows is not only the supreme moment of the opera but one of the supreme moments of all opera, comparable with the Quintet in Wagner's *The Mastersingers of Nuremberg* and incomparable as an example of writing for three soprano voices. Octavian softly sings ' Marie Theres'' while the orchestra holds a long chord, except for a solo trumpet which quietly plays [5]. Then, *moderato e molto cantabile*, the Marschallin sings the first high, floating phrase [46]. This melody is in fact just a transfiguration of Mariandel's ' *Nein, nein*' theme [40] from the supper-scene! Into the glowing, rich and immensely intricate vocal texture, the themes of [5] and [1] are interwoven. Each of the three soliloquises: Octavian about his love for Sophie; Sophie about the Marschallin and, at the end, as she looks into Octavian's eyes, about her own love; and the Marschallin about her renunciation of Octavian. The voices soar to a climax, and there is a glorious orchestral peroration based on [5], with Octavian's [1] on cellos and bassoons, and the silver rose music [28a and b] in the woodwind. With the enigmatic phrase ' *In Gottes Namen*' that suggests both her resignation and her blessing, the Marschallin quietly leaves.

The music of the Presentation of the Rose returns as Sophie and Octavian move closer to each other. Over a soft high tremolo, Sophie's [14] is repeated several times by oboe and flute while [1] spreads over the whole orchestra. They embrace and begin the chaste duet [47] which so perfectly complements the ardour of the Trio. (It may be compared with the Purcellian simplicity of the Fenton-Nannetta duet in Verdi's *Falstaff*.) To a recapitulation of the music with which she sent Octavian from her at the end of Act One, the Marschallin now re-enters with Faninal. ' *Sind halt aso, die jungen Leut*'' (*lit.*, 'That's how they are, the young folk'), Faninal sings benevolently. The Marschallin replies ' *Ja, Ja*'–and to those two notes the memorable interpreters of this rôle impart a whole world of experience, the strings at their sweetest telling us of the Marschallin's self-sacrifice. Alone again, Sophie and Octavian resume their duet, with each phrase underlined by the glittering [28b]. During an embrace Sophie drops her handkerchief. Their last words are sung to [29], with [28b] chiming out as they kiss and run out hand-in-hand. The stage is empty, and Strauss devises a codetta akin to the delicate epilogue of

Till Eulenspiegel. We hear Mahomet's tinkling bells [9]. The Marschallin has sent him back. Candle in hand he searches, finds the handkerchief and, waving it triumphantly, runs off to the accompaniment of brilliant, happy, final chords.

So ends an opera which, in its seventy years of existence, has already created its own mythology of interpreters of the various rôles, a mythology which the gramophone converts into reality for the listeners of today and tomorrow. Everything about it seems to have been blessed with the certainty of success. 'I pray you are content–for myself I must say I so enjoyed working on this piece that it almost saddens me to have to write "Curtain"', Hofmannsthal wrote to Strauss in 1910. And, when he was over eighty and had had many more triumphs, Richard Strauss was content to identify himself with the words, 'I am the composer of *Der Rosenkavalier*'.

Extracts from the Correspondence between Strauss and Hofmannsthal are quoted by kind permission of the Cambridge University Press, publishers of the English translation by Hanns Hammelmann and Ewald Osers.

Hugo von Hofmannsthal, an oil painting on wood, by Hans Schlesinger
(Courtesy of Octavian von Hofmannsthal)

Hugo von Hofmannsthal–Man of Letters

Peter Branscombe

Hugo von Hofmannsthal crammed a bewildering variety of activities into a comparatively short life. By the beginning of the last decade of the nineteenth century, when he was still in his mid teens, he was recognized as one of the most brilliant poetic talents in Vienna, already admitted to the circle around Hermann Bahr, Schnitzler (for whose *Anatol* he wrote the verse prologue) and Richard Beer-Hoffmann. He produced a quantity of lyric verse of a delicacy of perception and power of imagery that can perhaps be paralleled only by Rimbaud's rather earlier yet equally precocious poetry. But at the same time he was beginning to write a series of verse plays–plays for reading rather than for staging–such as *Gestern(Yesterday)*, *Der Tod des Tizian(The Death of Titian)* and *Der Tor und der Tod(The Fool and Death)*; before the decade was out there were nearly a dozen of them, including scenarios which were to become ballets with the music of Egon Wellesz (*Achilles auf Skyros*) and Zemlinsky (*Der Triumph der Zeit, The Triumph of Time*–though as composed by Zemlinsky it was named *Das gläserne Herz, The Heart of Glass*). The titles suggest the range of his interests at that time, just as the lyric poems indicate the uncanny insight he had acquired into the minds of people totally outside his own experience–a state of preternaturally mature understanding which he called *Praeexistenz* (literally ' pre-existence', referring to knowledge which must be assumed to have been acquired in a previous existence). The rich vein of poetic inspiration which he mined during the '90s ran out quite suddenly in the earliest years of the new century, shortly after he graduated Dr. phil. at Vienna with a thesis on linguistic usage in the group of sixteenth-century French poets known as the Pléiade.

It was at this stage in his career–1900, and he was 26–that he first came into contact with Richard Strauss. Initially, there can be little doubt, Hofmannsthal looked upon a possible collaboration with Germany's foremost musician as a solution to his own creative problems. However, for the moment Strauss declined the ballet-scenario *The Triumph of Time* which Hofmannsthal offered him, and their partnership did not begin until a few years later. Hofmannsthal sought to come to terms with his own problems of creativity and communication by adapting great works from the past, from various cultures. More intimately, he chose the extraordinary form of a fictitious letter from Lord Chandos to Francis Bacon (*Ein Brief – A Letter*) to express his own perception that words could no longer adequately convey a writer's meaning. Though this crisis was of comparatively short duration, the difficulties of communication were to remain an abiding concern of Hofmannsthal's, as they were at different times for such contrasting contemporaries as Wittgenstein, Kafka and Schönberg.

For the time being, however, he sought a solution to his artistic problems in the translation and adaptation of foreign dramatists, including Otway in *Das gerettete Venedig(Venice Preserved)*, and Sophocles in *Ödipus und die Sphinx* and *König Ödipus*. In 1906 his collaboration with Strauss began, after the composer had reacted enthusiastically to the Berlin production of Hofmannsthal's version of *Elektra* (in its original form as a spoken play). The poet was asked to make certain changes and cuts for Strauss's purposes–and the most productive partnership in the history of opera was born.

Although there is no precise dividing-line between his plays and his librettos, and indeed prose works and poems too as far as subject-matter is

Harold Barrett as the Marschallin's page in the first Covent Garden production, 1913. He later became a Stage Manager at the Royal Opera House. (Covent Garden Archives)

concerned, Hofmannsthal does tend to concentrate the attention in his opera-books on those aspects of femininity and of love which held a particular appeal for Strauss as well as for himself. The librettos explore the relationship between man and woman on various levels, and in two main thematic areas (the myth, and the sentimental comedy of manners). Even *Elektra*–which was not so much a collaboration between librettist and composer as the setting of an already-existing play–for all its insistence on the theme of vengeance, touches on the subject of love and child-bearing as the ideal of the gentle Chrysothemis. In the librettos after *Der Rosenkavalier* Hofmannsthal depicts love in a variety of ways. *Ariadne* reveals in the contrast between Ariadne and Zerbinetta, and the attraction between Ariadne and Bacchus, stylized forms of conventional operatic love. *The Woman without a Shadow* shows two pairs of lovers whose relationships are foundering on limited understanding–relationships that can only be made meaningful through self-sacrifice. Love in *The Egyptian Helen* is the spiritual resilience which is capable of surviving passing infatuation and the temptations of deception, and wins through to trust. *Arabella*, the last libretto Hofmannsthal lived to write (but did not live to revise and polish), shows up the incomplete nature of 'ordinary' human love when it is set against the perfect trust and generosity of spirit which Arabella and Mandryka finally achieve.

All these aspects of love are given vitality, directness and charm by Hofmannsthal's ability to fuse concept with language and gesture. Running through the librettos is, for instance, water-imagery. Chrysothemis uses the analogy of pregnant women struggling to bear water-pots from the well; water is the element over which Bacchus, greeted as if he were Charon, comes to bring not death but renewed life and love to Ariadne; in *The Woman without a Shadow* water plays an unusually large role, both in points of detail and in the final tableau, with a golden stream cascading before the re-united couples as promise of fruitfulness; *Arabella* takes from Slav folksong the motif of the glass of pure water given to her future husband by the bride.

Another recurrent theme connected with love is the creation of a meaningful family unit (for Hofmannsthal increasingly a vital concern in the chaotic years of European political and social disintegration). It is the message of the beautiful comedy *Der Schwierige* (*The Difficult Man*), as it is of the roughly contemporaneous *Woman without a Shadow*. The decision of Hans-Karl, the 'difficult man' of the play's title, virtually to retire from society and remove to his estate with Helene can be viewed as escapism; yet in the circumstances of post-war Austria, Hofmannsthal was as convinced as Stifter had been after the 1848 Revolution that the future of society at large was dependent on the unit of the family. Lest the accusation that the poet was advocating escapism should nevertheless stick, it should be pointed out that in his final play, *Der Turm* (*The Tower*), he probed the disquieting political realities of the '20s, set in a central European mythical-historical context. Here for the last time he reworked a powerful foreign work–Calderón's *La vida es sueño* (*Life is a Dream*) so as to cast fresh light on the recurrent problems of sifting permanent from transient values, of fostering the resilient, self-sacrificing spirit of true humanity in a world heavy with corruption.

One may also see Hofmannsthal's concern for international understanding, for the need to transmit the basic values of civilization, in his determined work with Max Reinhardt and others after the First World War to establish the Salzburg Festival as a meeting-place for artists and art-lovers at which works of eminence from past and present should be given in exemplary performances, and by which better understanding between nations should be encouraged. This principle underlies many of his adaptations– *Jedermann* (his version of the old English morality play of *Everyman*) before the War, after the War *Das grosse Salzburger Welttheater* (*The Great Salzburg Theatre of the World*). The latter, though less inextricably a part of the Salzburg Festival than *Jedermann*, is the more ambitious play, with its parabolic reflection of the dark forces at work in Europe, and its emphasis on individual responsibility if chaos is to be averted.

From the conscious and admitted adaptations it is fascinating to turn to the hidden literary borrowings, more or less conscious memories of his passionate and voracious reading in several languages; antecedents of the most varied kind can be found for a vast number of tiny details in his writings. Yet these borrowings are so creative, his use of them so subtle, that the accusation that he was a kleptomaniac has only the most superficial application. Hofmannsthal was equally likely to draw his inspiration from a novel or a folksong, a play or a myth, a volume of memoirs or a history book; on occasion he adapted a scene from a painting (Hogarth's 'Levée' in *Rosenkavalier*, Act One), or even modelled a character on an acquaintance (Strauss's wife was the prototype for the Empress in *Die Frau ohne Schatten*). The immediacy of his character-depiction clearly owes much to his loving compilation of detail; even minor characters come vividly to life.

Hofmannsthal's concern with the problem of communication is of crucial importance throughout his life, and may be studied in such disparate and chronologically widely separated works as the early lyric poem, *Die Beiden*, *Der Schwierige* (for instance in the scene in which Hans-Karl tries to propose marriage), and the preface to the volume of essays *Wert und Ehre deutscher Sprache* (literally, 'Worth and Honour of the German Language') two years before his death, in which he hoped by pointing to treasures from Germany's literary past to help young people come to a proper understanding of the need to preserve the spirit of the German language. Problems of communication— of winning through to a mature understanding of the nature of another person—also play an important part within the librettos: in *Elektra* it is the relationship between the protagonist and her brother and sister; in *Der Rosenkavalier* between Octavian and the Marschallin, Octavian and Sophie; in *Ariadne* the focus is on Ariadne and Bacchus, but also on artist and public, artist and artist. *The Woman without a Shadow* focuses attention on the lack of insight between the two couples, in *The Egyptian Helen* the concern is for the relationship between the long-separated husband and wife, and in *Arabella* it is for the engaged couple who must rise above misunderstandings.

Not the least interesting aspect of the Hofmannsthal-Strauss partnership is the choice of subjects they finally made and followed through to successful conclusion, and the subjects proposed and temporarily pursued by the one, but rejected by the other. It is curious to think we might have had a Hofmannsthal-Strauss *Semiramis*, odder still to think what a Hofmannsthal-Strauss *Intermezzo* might have been like. Strauss also tried to wheedle out of the poet a libretto on a French Revolution subject, or something lurid from the Italian Renaissance. To these and similar requests Hofmannsthal could only just keep a note of censure from the wording of his refusal. Nor was Strauss always keen to follow Hofmannsthal in his inclinations, *Christinas Heimreise*, a play based on an incident from Casanova's life being one example, and a proposed ballet on the subject of Orestes and the Furies another. The fact that there was tension and disagreement in the working relationship was surely to its advantage—neither of the collaborators was able or indeed willing entirely to submerge his own artistic personality in the interests of the other. Each made sacrifices, but it was Hofmannsthal, the more delicate of the partners, who was better able—thanks not least to his intellectual toughness and resilience—to maintain his own independent creative development during the years of their co-operation, as the impressive list of works written for his own rather than Strauss's purposes indicates.

In the letter he wrote to congratulate Strauss on his sixtieth birthday, in June 1924, Hofmannsthal remarked that it seemed to him to be 'something great and also necessary in my life that you approached me, eighteen years ago now, with your wishes and needs. It was pre-ordained that I am able to fulfil this wish—within the limitations of my talents—and that this fulfilment should in turn satisfy an inner need in me . . . . You have rewarded me as far as one artist can reward another. . . '. A further reward, which Hofmannsthal did not live to see, is that his example of providing a corpus of dignified, poetic librettos has helped contemporaries and successors of such varied outlooks as Brecht, Cocteau, Busoni, E.M. Forster, Ingeborg Bachmann, Christopher Fry, Gertrude Stein, Auden and Kallman (whose *Elegy for Young Lovers* is dedicated to Hofmannsthal's memory) to perceive the worth of operatic collaboration.

36

Frieda Hempel as the Marschallin and Margaret Ober as Octavian in the American première at the Met., December 9, 1913.

Left. The first performance: Eva von der Osten (Octavian) and Margarethe Siems (the Marschallin) in the 1911 Dresden production.

Below. The same scene at Covent Garden in 1975 with Brigitte Fassbaender (Octavian) and Gwyneth Jones (the Marschallin), in Visconti's production. (photo: Donald Southern)

Thematic Guide

Many of the themes from the opera have been identified in the articles by numbers in square brackets, which refer to the themes set out on these pages. The themes are also identified by the numbers in brackets at the corresponding points in the libretto, so that the words can be related to the musical themes.

[7]

A tempo mosso

p espressivo

[8]

Allegro

[9a]

Alla marcia con grazia

[9b]

Alla marcia con grazia

[10]

Tempo di Waltz

[11]

Vivo

[12]

Pesante

[13]

Commodo

[14]

 [15]

Con moto

[16]

Tempo di Waltz

[17] OCHS

Presto

Is that a - ny rea - son to live like a monk?
Macht das ei - nem leh - men E - sel aus mir?

[18]

Presto

[19] THE ITALIAN TENOR

Un poco sostenuto

Di ri - go - ri ar - ma - to il se - no

41

[20]

Allegro non troppo

[21]

Vivace possibile

[22]

Con moto

[23] **MARSCHALLIN**

Più tranquillo

For time, how strange-ly, goes its own way
Die Zeit, die ist ein son-der-bar Ding.

[24]

Molto allegro

[25]

Moderato

[26]

[27] **SOPHIE**

On this most joy — ful day I praise thee my ma - ker
In die - ser fei — er - li - chen Stun - de der Prü - fung

[28a]

Piuttosto lento

[28b]

[29] **SOPHIE**

Where have I been be - fore _____ and felt such rap - ture?
Wo war ich schon ein - mal _____ und war so se - lig?

[30] **SOPHIE**

Animato grazioso

I know you ve - ry well, mon cou - sin!
Ich kenn' Ihn schon recht wohl, mon cou - sin!

[31]

Tempo di Waltz tranquillo

[32]

43

[33] *The Luck of the Lerchenaus*

Waltz mosso

[34] **SOPHIE**

Andante mosso

My trust is in your kind - ness _____ mon cou - sin,
Zu Ihm hätt' ich ein Zu - traum, _____ mon cou - sin,

[35] ·OCTAVIAN

Cantabile

With eyes all veiled by your tears you're ask - ing my aid,__
Mit Ih - ren Au - gen voll Trä - nen kommt Sie zu mir,__

[36]

[37]

Tempo di Waltz *con anima*

[38]

Tempo di Valse
con spirito

44

[39]

Molto animato

[40] OCTAVIAN

Un poco languido

No, no, let be No wine for me.
Nein, nein, nein, nein I trink kein Wein.

[41]

Tempo di Waltz *con grazia*

[42]

Waltz un poco commodo

[43] OCTAVIAN

Moderato assai

'Tis all one, 'tis all one,
Es is ja eh alls eins,

45

[44]

Molto allegro sempre

[45] OCTAVIAN

Moderato

Eh bien, ___ have you no friend - ly word for me?
Eh bien, ___ hat Sie kein freund - lich Wort für mich?

[46] MARSCHALLIN *(Trio)*

Moderato e molto cantabile

I ___ made a vow to love_____ him right - ly
Hab' ___ mir's ge - lobt, ihn lieb_____ zu ha - ben

[47] SOPHIE, OCTAVIAN

Andante tranquillo

S.
Am I dream- ing that here we stand, one in happ - i -ness and
Ist ein traum kann nicht wirk- lich sein, dass wir zwei bei - ei

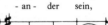

O.
Bliss too deep to un - der - stand one in happ - i -ness and
Spür mich dich, spür' nur dich, al - lein und dass wir - bei - ein -

hand in hand,
- an - der sein,

hand in hand!
an - der sein!

46

Der Rosenkavalier

Comedy for Music in Three Acts

by Hugo von Hofmannsthal
Music by Richard Strauss
English version by Alfred Kalisch

This libretto has been laid out following Hofmannsthal's original instructions, including many elaborate stage directions which do not necessarily reflect any ENO or other modern production. Alfred Kalisch's translation, which dates from 1913, has been very considerably amended in the course of performances, as is inevitable with any performing translation. The square brackets indicate words in the text which Strauss never set to music; the numbers in square brackets refer to the thematic guide.

The opera is often extensively cut in performance, notably Baron Ochs's Act One speeches, his monologue after the duel in the second act, and various choruses and exchanges in the third act.

Der Rosenkavalier was first performed in Dresden on January 26, 1911. The first performance in Britain was given at Covent Garden on January 29, 1913, and in New York on December 9 of the same year. On March 8, 1939, there was a production in English by Sadler's Wells Opera at Sadler's Wells Theatre. The first performance of the current ENO production took place at the London Coliseum on January 29, 1975.

THE CHARACTERS

The Feldmarschallin *Princess of Werdenberg*	soprano
Octavian *called Quinquin, a young gentleman of noble family*	soprano
The Princess's Footmen	2 tenors, 2 basses
Baron Ochs of Lerchenau	bass
Major-Domo to the Princess	tenor
A Noble Widow	mezzo-soprano
Three Noble Orphans	2 sopranos 1 mezzo-soprano
A Milliner	soprano
An Animal Seller	tenor
A Notary	bass
Valzacchi *an intriguer*	tenor
Annina *his accomplice*	mezzo-soprano
A Tenor	tenor
Herr von Faninal *a rich merchant, newly ennobled*	baritone
Sophie *his daughter*	soprano
Marianne Leitmetzerin *Sophie's Duenna*	soprano
Major-Domo to Faninal	tenor
A Doctor	bass
A Landlord	tenor
A Commissar of Police	baritone

Pages to the Princess and Octavian, Hairdressers, a Flute Player, Leopold and Ochs's Retinue, Waiters, a Scholar, a Cook and Assistant, Notary's Assistant, Maidservants, Footmen, Suspicious Personages, Children, Musicians, Coachmen and Constables.

The action takes place in Vienna, during the first years of the reign of Maria Theresa.

Act One

Introduction [1, 2, 3, 4, 5, 6] *The Marschallin's bedroom. To the left in the alcove the large tent-shaped four poster. Next to the bed, a three-leaved Chinese screen, behind which some clothes are lying. In addition, a little table and some chairs. On a little sofa to the left lies a sword in its sheath. To the right, great folding doors leading to the antechamber. In the centre, scarcely visible, a small door in the wall. No other doors. Between the alcove and the small door a dressing table and a few armchairs against the wall. The curtains of the bed are half-drawn. Through the half-open window the bright morning sun streams in. From the garden bird-song can be heard.*

Octavian kneels on a footstool, half embracing the Marschallin who is reclining in bed. Her face is hidden; only her beautiful hand and arm, peeping out from the sleeve of her lace nightgown, can be seen.

OCTAVIAN
(*passionately*)

I alone! None but I	[7] Wie Du warst! Wie Du bist!
Know the treasures of your kindness!	Das weiss niemand, das ahnt Keiner!

MARSCHALLIN
(*raises herself on her pillow*)

Do your reproach me for that, Quinquin?	Beklagt Er sich über das, Quin-quin?
Would you have all the world share them?	Möcht' Er, dass viele das wüssten?

OCTAVIAN
(*ardently*)

Angel! No! Blessed am I,	Engel! Nein! Selig bin ich,
For it is I alone know all your secrets!	Das ich der Einzige bin, der weiss, wie Du bist.
All your secrets! All your treasures!	Keiner ahnt es! Niemand weiss es!
You, you, you—Why speak of "you"?	Du, Du, Du—was heisst das "Du"?
This "You and me"?	Was "Du und ich"?
Do we know what they mean?	Hat denn das einen Sinn?
These are words, merely words—Yes—	Das sind Wörter, blosse Wörter, nicht?
You know.	Du sag'.
All the same though, there is something	Aber dennoch: Es ist etwas in ihnen,
within them, a feeling, a craving,	ein Schwindeln, ein Ziehen, ein Sehnen
a yearning, a striving,	und Drängen,
A longing, a burning:	ein Schmachten und Brennen:
My hand reaches out to search for your hand,	Wie jetzt meine Hand zu Deiner Hand kommt,
And I must touch you, I want to hold you.	Das Zu-Dir-wollen, das Dich-umklammern
All I want is only you;	das bin ich, das will zu Dir;
But then I am lost in that "You" ...	aber das Ich vergeht in dem Du ...
I am your heart—but then when I	Ich bin Dein Bub—aber wenn mir dann
am carried away in your arms—	Hören und Sehen vergeht—
Where is then your heart?	wo ist dann Dein Bub?

MARSCHALLIN
(*softly*)

You are my heart, you are my love!	Du bist mein Bub, Du bist mein Schatz!

(*very tenderly*)

I love you so!	Ich hab' Dich lieb!

(*They embrace.*) [6]

OCTAVIAN
(*starts up*)

Why is it day? It shall not be day!	Warum ist Tag? Ich will nicht den Tag!
What use is the day?	Für was ist der Tag?
Then everyone sees you. Dark it shall be.	Da haben Dich alle! Finster soll sein!

(*He rushes to the window, closes it, and draws the curtains; the distant tinkling of a bell is heard. The Marschallin laughs to herself.*) [8]

OCTAVIAN

Why do you laugh?	Lachst Du mich aus?

49

	MARSCHALLIN
	(*tenderly*)
Why do I laugh?	Lach 'ich Dich aus?
	OCTAVIAN
Angel!	Engel!
	MARSCHALLIN
Dearest, my sweetest love!	Schatz Du, mein junger Schatz!

(*again a discreet tinkling*)

	MARSCHALLIN
Hark!	Horch!
	OCTAVIAN
I will not.	Ich will nicht.
	MARSCHALLIN
Quiet, be still!	Still, pass auf!
	OCTAVIAN
I will not listen! What can it be?	Ich will nichts hören! Was wird's denn sein?

(*The sound comes closer.*)

Is it footmen with letters, and pretty verses?	Sind's leicht Laufer mit Briefen und Komplimenten?
From Saurau, from Hartig, or the Portuguese Ambassador?	Vom Saurau, vom Hartig, von Portugieser Envoyé?
Here no-one enters but I! I am master here! [1]	Hier kommt keiner herein. Hier bin ich der Herr!

(*The little door at the centre opens and a little Black Boy in yellow, hung with silver bells, trips across the room bearing a salver with chocolate. Invisible hands close the door behind him.*)

	MARSCHALLIN
Quick, go and hide yourself, for breakfast comes.	Schnell, da versteck' Er sich! Das Frühstück ist's.

(*Octavian steps behind the screen.*)

	MARSCHALLIN
Take your sword, put it there behind the bed.	Schmeiss Er doch Seinen Degen hinter's Bett.

(*Octavian makes a dash for his sword and hides it. The Marschallin lies down again, after drawing the curtains. The Black Boy places the tray on the little table, pushes it to the front of the stage, pulls up the sofa and makes a deep obeisance to the Marschallin, with his arms crossed over his chest. Then he dances daintily backwards, with his face always turned to the Marschallin. At the door he bows again and vanishes. [9] The Marschallin appears from behind the bed curtains. She has wrapped a light fur-trimmed dressing-gown around her. Octavian reappears between the wall and the screen.*)

	MARSCHALLIN
You scatterbrain! What were you thinking of?	Er Katzenkopf! Er Unvorsichtiger!
Gentlemen do not leave their swords lying in the room of a lady of fashion.	Lässt man in einer Dame Schlafzimmer seinen Degen herumliegen?
You should go to school again to learn your manners.	Hat Er keine Besseren Gepflogenheiten?
	OCTAVIAN
But if my manners are not to your taste, [1]	Wenn Ihr zu dumm ist, wie ich mich benehm'
If it offends you that I've no experience in matters such as this,	und wenn Ihr abgeht, dass ich kein Geübter in solchen Sachen bin,
Why then, I have no notion how to please.	dan weiss ich überhaupt nicht, was Sie an mir hat!
	MARSCHALLIN
	(*tenderly, from the sofa*)
Now don't philosophize, my Love, and come to me.	Philosphier' Er nicht, Herr Schatz und komm' Er her.
Now let's have breakfast. Everything in its own time.	Jetzt wird gefrühstückt. Jedes Ding hat seine Zeit.

50

(Octavian seats himself beside her. They are very tender over breakfast. Octavian buries his face in her lap. She strokes his hair. He looks up at her.) [10]

OCTAVIAN
(softly)

Marie Theres'! [4] Marie Theres'!

MARSCHALLIN

Octavian! Octavian!

OCTAVIAN

Bichette! Bichette!

MARSCHALLIN

Quinquin! Quinquin!

OCTAVIAN

My heart! Mein Schatz!

MARSCHALLIN

My love! Mein Bub!
(They continue breakfast.)

OCTAVIAN
(merrily)

The Feldmarschall is in Franconian woods and hunts for bear there and wild boar.	Der Feldmarschall sitzt im crowatischen Wald und jagt auf Bären und Luchsen.
And I, I stay here in all my youth, and hunt for what?	Und ich, ich sitz hier, ich junges Blut undjag' auf was?
Ah, what joy! Ah, what joy!	Ich hab' ein Glück, ich hab' ein Glück!

MARSCHALLIN
(a shadow flitting across her face)

Oh leave the Feldmarschall in peace!	Lass Er den Feldmarschall in Ruh'!
I dreamt of him last night.	Mir hat von ihm geträumt.

OCTAVIAN

Last night! You dreamt of him last night? Last night?	Heut' Nacht hat Dir von ihm geträumt? Heut' Nacht?

MARSCHALLIN

My dreams, they are not mine to command. Ich schaff' mir meine Träume nicht an.

OCTAVIAN

Do you mean you really dreamt of him last night? Last night?	Heute Nacht hat Dir von Deinem Mann geträumt? Heut' Nacht?

MARSCHALLIN

Don't stare so, don't be angry, it's no fault of mine.	Mach'Er nicht solche Augen. Ich kann nichts dafür.
I dreamt that he came home again.	Er war [auf] einmal wieder zu Haus.

OCTAVIAN
(softly)

The Feldmarschall? Der Feldmarschall?

MARSCHALLIN

There was a noise below of horse and hound, and you were here.	Es war ein Lärm im Hof von Pferd' und Leut' und Er war da.
With fright I started up in haste. Ah, look now,	Vor Schreck war ich auf einmal wach, nein schau nur,
See just what a child I am: I still can hear it, all the noise below.	schau nur, wie ich kindisch bin: ich hör' noch immer den Rumor im Hof.
It's ringing in my ears. Don't you hear something?	Ich bring's nicht aus dem Ohr. Hörst Du leicht auch was?

OCTAVIAN

Yes, something I can hear, but why should it be your husband?	Ja freilich hör' ich was, aber muss es denn Dein Mann sein!?
Only think a moment, he's far away now, hunting in the mountains.	Denk' Dir doch, wo der ist im Raitzenland noch hinterwärts von Esseg.

MARSCHALLIN

Is it really so far?	Ist das sicher sehr weit?
Then what we hear is something else. And all is well.	Na dann wird's halt was anders sein. Dan is ja gut.

OCTAVIAN

You seem so anxious still, Theres'.   Du schaust so ängstlich drein, Theres'!

MARSCHALLIN

Listen, Quinquin, although he's far away,   Weiss Er, Quinquin—wenn es auch weit ist—

The Feldmarschall can travel like the wind.   Der Feldmarschall is halt sehr geschwind.
For once...   Einmal—

(She pauses.)

OCTAVIAN

What happened once?   Was war einmal?

(The Marschallin listens, abstractedly.)

OCTAVIAN
(jealously)

What happened once? Bichette,   Was war einmal? Bichette!
Bichette, what happened once?   Bichette! Was war einmal?

MARSCHALLIN

Ah, do be good, leave my poor heart its secrets.   Ach sei Er gut, Er muss nicht alles wissen.

OCTAVIAN

You trifle with my heart!   So spielt sie sich mit mir!
(He throws himself in despair onto the sofa.)
I am a poor miserable wretch!   Ich bin ein unglücklicher Mensch!

MARSCHALLIN
(listening)

Do calm yourself. Be quiet.   Jetzt trotz' Er nicht. Jetzt gilt's:
  It is the Feldmarschall.   Es ist der Feldmarschall.
For, were a stranger there, the noise would   Wenn es ein Fremder wär', so wär' der
  surely be out there in my antechamber.   Lärm da draussen in meinem Vorzimmer.
It is my husband, now stamping up the   Es muss mein Mann sein, der durch die
  private staircase,   Garderob' herein will
And forcing the footmen to give way.   Und mit den Lakaien disputiert.
Quinquin, my husband's here!   Quinquin, es ist mein Mann!

(Octavian draws his sword and runs to the right.)

MARSCHALLIN

Not there; that is the antechamber.   Nicht dort, das ist das Vorzimmer.
There sits a crowd of my dependents and   Da sitzen meine Lieferanten und ein halbes
  a score of lackeys waiting.   Dutzend Lakaien.
There!   Da!

(Octavian runs to the small door.)

MARSCHALLIN

Too late! They're coming up the private   Zu spät! Sie sind schon in der Garde-
  stairs.   rob'!
One chance remains,   Jetzt bleibt nur eins!
Go hide yourself!   Versteck Er sich!
(after a brief pause of indecision)
There!   Dort!

OCTAVIAN

I will not let him pass! I stay by you!   Ich spring' ihm in den Weg! Ich bleib' bei Dir.

MARSCHALLIN

There by the bed! There in the curtains!   Dort hinter's Bett! Dort in die Vorhäng'.
And do not move!   Und rühr' Dich nicht!

OCTAVIAN
(hesitating)

If I am caught, what will become of you,   Wenn er mich dort erwischt, was wird aus
  Theres'?   Dir, Theres'?

MARSCHALLIN
(pleading)

Hide quickly now, my love.   Versteck Er sich, mein Schatz.

OCTAVIAN
(by the screen)

Theres'!   Theres'!

(He vanishes between the screen and the alcove wall.)

52

MARSCHALLIN
(stamping her feet impatiently)

Only stay still!	Sei Er ganz still!

(with flashing eyes)

Now we shall see	Das möcht ich seh'n,
If he dares to force his way inside while I am here.	Ob einer sich dort hinüber traut, wenn ich hier steh'.
I'm no faint-hearted Italian Brigadier: Where I stand I stand.	Ich bin kein napolitanischer General: wo ich steh' steh' ich.

(She goes with determination to the small door and listens.)

They're worthy fellows standing outside there. They will not let him in to me.	Sind brave Kerl'n, meine Lakaien, wollen ihn nicht herein lassen,
Saying I'm asleep! Most worthy fellows!	sagen, dass ich schlaf'. Sehr brave Kerl'n.

(The noise outside grows louder. She listens.)

That voice!	Die Stimm'!
That is not, surely, that's not my husband's voice!	Das ist ja gar nicht die Stimm' vom Feldmarschall!
They're saying "Herr Baron" to him. It is a stranger.	Sie sagen "Herr Baron" zu ihm! Das ist ein Fremder.

(gaily)

Quinquin, it is someone else.	Quinquin, es ist ein Besuch.

(She laughs.)

Soon escape will be quite easy,	Fahr' Er schnell in seine Kleider
But in hiding remain,	aber bleib' Er versteckt,
So that the footmen do not see you.	dass die Lakaien Ihn nicht seh'n.
That foolish, loutish voice, surely it's familiar.	Die blöde grosse Stimm' müsste ich doch kennen.
Who can it be? My God, it surely is Ochs,	Wer ist denn das? Herrgott, das ist der Ochs.
It is my cousin of Lerchenau, it's Ochs of Lerchenau.	Das ist mein Vetter, der Lerchenau, der Ochs aus Lerchenau.
What does he want? Heavens above us!	Was will denn der? Jesus Maria!

(She laughs.)

Quinquin, listen.	Quinquin, hört Er?
Quinquin, you cannot have forgot,	Quinquin, erinnert Er sich nicht?
One day a letter was brought—	Vor fünf [oder] sechs Tagen—den Brief—
We were alone in my carriage—	Wir sind im Wagen gesessen
And someone came galloping up with a letter in his hand.	und einen Brief haben sie mir an den Wagenschlag gebracht.
That letter came from Ochs;	Das war der Brief vom Ochs.
And now I have entirely forgotten what it said.	Und ich hab' keine Ahnung, was drin gestanden ist.

(She laughs.)

And it is you who were guilty, Quinquin.	Daran ist Er allein Schuld, Quinquin.

VOICE OF THE MAJOR-DOMO
(outside)

Herr Baron, will you be pleased to wait in the gallery.	Beliebden Euer Gnaden in der Gallerie zu warten!

(During the next speeches the small doors at the back are pulled ajar several times and shut again, as if someone outside was trying to force his way in, and someone else was preventing him.)

VOICE OF THE BARON
(outside)

Where did you learn such manners as these?	Wo hat Er seine Manieren gelernt?
Herr Baron Lerchenau can't be kept waiting.	Der Baron Lerchenau antichambrieret nicht.

MARSCHALLIN

Quinquin, where are you now? Where have you gone?	Quinquin, was treibt Er denn? Vo steckt Er denn?

OCTAVIAN
(coming out in a skirt and short jacket, his hair bound with a kerchief and ribbon, and making a curtsey) [11]

Your ladyship's servant! I've not been long in your Highness's household here.	Befehl'n fürstli' Gnad'n I bin halt, noch nit recht lang in fürstli'n Dienst.

You dear.	Du, Schatz!
And only one kiss may I give you.	Und nicht einmal mehr als ein Busserl
That's for your wages.	kann ich Dir geben.

(*She kisses him quickly. There is more noise outside.*)

He's hammering the door down, my dear cousin.	Er bricht mir ja die Tür ein, der Herr Vetter.
Now, as quickly as may be,	Mach Er, dass Er hinauskomm'.
Boldly march by all the footmen there.	Schlief' Er frech durch die Lakaien durch.
It's sport for brazen rogues like you!	Er ist ein blitzgescheidter Lump! Und
And soon come back, my love,	komm' Er wieder, Schatz.
But in men's clothing and through the main	Aber in Mannskleidern und durch die
gate, whene'er you like.	vord're Tür, wenn's Ihm beliebt.

(*She sits down on the sofa on the left with her back to the door and begins to drink her chocolate. Octavian hurries to the small door and tries to leave by it, but at the same moment the door is flung open, and Baron Ochs enters, the footmen trying in vain to keep him back. Octavian lowers his head and tries to escape quickly, but collides with him, and backs up to the wall on the left in confusion. Three footmen have entered with the Baron, and stand at a loss.*)

BARON
(*pompously to the footmen*)

I'm quite certain Her Highness will receive me.	Selbstverständlich empfängt [mich] Ihre Gnaden.

(*He comes forward, while the footmen on his left try to bar his passage.*) [12]

BARON
(*to Octavian with interest*)

Pardon, my pretty child.	Pardon, mein hübsches Kind!

(*Octavian in confusion turns his face to the wall.*)

BARON
(*graciously and with condescension*)

I said, "Pardon, my pretty child".	Ich sag': Pardon, mein hübsches Kind.

(*The Marschallin looks over her shoulder, rises, and goes to meet the Baron, who addresses Octavian gallantly.*)

I hope I did not really frighten you.	Ich hab' Ihr doch nicht ernstlich weh getan?

THE THREE FOOTMEN
(*attracting the Baron's attention, softly*)

Her Most Excellent Highness!	Ihre fürstlichen Gnaden!

(*They take up their position in a tight row near the Marschallin, right in front of the small doors. The Baron makes an obeisance in the French manner, repeating it twice.*)

MARSCHALLIN

My dear Cousin, you're looking well today.	Euer Liebden sehen vortrefflich aus.

BARON
(*bows again, then to the footmen*)

See what I told you, she is simply delighted that I came.	Sieht Er jetzt wohl, dass Ihre Gnaden entzückt ist, mich zu seh'n.

(*The Baron goes towards the Marschallin with the bearing of a man of the world, giving her his hand and leading her forward.*)

(*quietly*)

And why should Your Highness not be glad!	Und wie sollten Euer Gnaden nicht!
Time is so unimportant when one's a person of rank.	Was tut die frühe Stunde unter Personen von Stand?
Have I not morning after morning	Hab' ich nicht seinerzeit wahrhaftig Tag für Tag
Visited our dear Princess Brioche, just to pay my respects to her,	uns'rer Fürstin Brioche meine Aufwartung gemacht,
While in her bath she sat at ease,	da sie im Bad gesessen ist,
With nothing except a tiny silk screen between her and me?	mit nichts als einem kleinen Wandschirm zwischen ihr und mir.
I am astounded [13]	Ich muss mich wundern

(*looking angrily around*)

that any lackey dare—	wenn Euer Gnaden Livree—

54

(Octavian would like to have slipped out in the meantime; the astonished glances of the footmen force him to be extremely cautious, and with affected ease he makes his way along the wall to the alcove.)

MARSCHALLIN

Forgive them, please,	Verzeihen Sie.
My orders were given, they have obeyed them.	Man hat sich betragen, wie es befohlen [war].
I suffered this morning from a headache.	Ich hatte diesen Morgen die Migräne.

(At a sign from the Marschallin, the footmen have brought the two small sofas forward and retired. Octavian busies himself about the bed as inconspicuously as possible. The Marschallin seats herself on the sofa on the right after offering the Baron the sofa on the left.)

BARON

(trying to sit down, much distracted by the presence of the pretty maid. Aside)

A pretty wench! A tasty, saucy baggage!	Ein hübsches Ding! Ein gutes saub'res Kinderl!

(The Marschallin rises and ceremoniously again offers him a seat. The Baron seats himself with hesitation, trying not to turn his back completely on the pretty maid. In the ensuing dialogue he turns sometimes towards the Marschallin, on his left, and sometimes to Octavian, on his right.)

MARSCHALLIN

And even now I'm not quite well.	Ich bin auch jetzt noch [nicht] ganz wohl.
My dear Cousin, bearing that in mind, will have the kindness—	Der Vetter wird darum vielleicht die Gnade haben—

BARON

Why surely.	Natürlich.

(He turns to his right to look at Octavian.)

MARSCHALLIN

It's my waiting woman, a young girl from the country.	Meine Kammerzofe, ein junges Ding vom Lande.
I'm afraid, though, her manners may not please your Lordship.	Ich muss fürchten, die incommodiert Euer Liebden.

BARON

(facing right)

She's very sweet!	Ganz allerliebst!

(facing left)

What? She does not please me! Me? The contrary!	Wie? Nicht im Geringsten! Mich? Im Gegenteil!

(He beckons Octavian with his hand. Then to the Marschallin)

But Your Highness perhaps was surprised to learn that I'm to be a bridegroom—	Euer Gnaden werden vielleicht verwundert sein, das ich als Bräutigam—

(looking to his left)

but yet, meanwhile—	indess—inzwischen—

MARSCHALLIN

A bridegroom?	Als Bräutigam?

BARON

(to his left)

Yes, I wrote it all in the letter that I sent to Your Highness—	Ja, Euer Gnaden, denn doch [wol] aus meinem Brief genugsam—

(to his right)

A rascal, very juicy, just a babe in arms.	Ein Grasaff', appetitlich, keine fünfzehn Jahr!

MARSCHALLIN

(relieved)

You wrote a letter. Why of course, and who's the lucky bride to be?	Der Brief, natürlich, ja, der Brief, wer ist denn nur die Glückliche?
I have forgotten for the moment.	Ich hab' den Namen auf der Zunge.

BARON

(to his left)

Eh?	Wie?

(over his shoulder)

Fresh as paint! So clean! So healthy! What a wench!	Pudeljung! Gesund! Gewaschen! Allerliebst!

55

MARSCHALLIN

But tell me who's the bride?	**MARSCHALLIN** Wer ist nur schnell die Braut?
Sophie Faninal. But Your Highness, I did not keep her name a secret.	**BARON** [14] Das Fräulein Faninal. [Ich] habe Euer Gnaden den Namen nicht verheimlicht.
Forgive me. My memory is at fault. What of Her family? They do not come from here?	**MARSCHALLIN** Natürlich. Wo hab' ich meinen Kopf? Bloss die Famili ist mir nicht bekannt. Sind's keine Hiesigen?

(*Octavian busies himself with the tray, and thus gets behind the Baron.*)

I assure Your Highness, they do come from here. One which Her Majesty the Queen has raised to noble rank. They have the contract now for the supplies of all our armies in the West.	**BARON** Jawohl, Euer Gnaden, es sind Hiesige. Ein durch die Gnade Ihre Majestät Geadelter. Er hat die Lieferung für die Armee, die in den Niederlanden steht.

(*The Marschallin makes impatient signs to Octavian to withdraw.*)

BARON
(completely misunderstanding her expression)

I see that Your Highness shows upon her brow disdain at the misalliance. And yet, although I say it, the girl's as pretty as an angel from above. She comes straight from a convent. She's an only child.	Ich seh', Euer Gnaden runzeln Dero Schöne Stirn ob der Mesalliance. Allein, dass ich es sage, das Mädchen ist für einen Engel hübsch genug. Kommt frischwegs aus dem Kloster. Ist das einzige Kind,

(more emphatically)

Her father possesses twelve houses in the city and has a palace too. He's not over healthy,	Den Mann gehören zwölf Häuser auf der Wied'n nebst dem Palais am Hof. Und seine Gesundheit—

(chuckling)

—or so I've heard it said.	—soll nicht die beste sein.

Ah, my dear Cousin, I can see now which way the wind is blowing.	**MARSCHALLIN** Mein lieber Vetter, ich capier' schon, wieviel's geschlagen hat.

(*She signals to Octavian to withdraw.*)

And if Your Highness will allow me, It seems to me I come of such a highly born and noble family that you can say My blood is blue enough for two, Corpo di bacco! I'll see to it that the social standing that my wife should have, She'll have without a question, and as regards our children, if the Queen should refuse them the golden keys of nobility—Va bene! They'll still possess the twelve iron keys To their twelve houses in the city for their consolation.	**BARON** Und mit Verlaub [von Euer] fürstlichen Gnaden ich dünke mir, gut's adeliges Blut genug im Leib zu haben für ihrer Zwei: man bleibt doch schliesslich was man ist, Corpo di bacco! Den Vortritt, wo er ihr gebührt, wird man der Frau Gemahlin noch zu verschaffen wissen, und was die Kinder anlangt, wenn sie denen den goldnen Schlüssel nicht concedieren werden—Va bene! Sie werden sich mit den zwölf eisernen Schlüsseln zu den zwölf Häusern auf der Wied'n zu getrösten wissen.

Of course. I'm sure no child of yours would ever find it hard to endure such consolation.	**MARSCHALLIN** Gewiss! O sicherlich dem Vetter seine Kinder, die werden keine Don Quixotten [sein]!

(*Octavian walks backwards with the tray towards the door.*)

56

Where are you going with that chocolate? Warum hinaus die Chocolade! Geruhen
  Come back here now! nur!
Wait! Pst, what is it? Da! Pst, wieso denn!

(*Octavian hesitates, averting his face.*)

MARSCHALLIN

Off with you now! Fort, geh' Sie nur!

BARON

If you will allow me, Your Highness, Wenn ich Euer Gnaden gestehe
I haven't had a bite today. dass ich [noch] so gut wie nüchtern bin.

MARSCHALLIN
(*resignedly*)

Mariandl, bring it back, and wait upon his Mariandl, komm' sie her. Servier' Sie
  Lordship. Seiner Liebden.
(*Octavian comes back and serves the Baron from his right, so that the latter is again between
the Marschallin and Octavian.*)

BARON
(*taking a cup and helping himself*)

I'm nearly starving, my dear Cousin. So gut wie nüchtern, Euer Gnaden. Sitz' im
  Sitting in my carriage since five o'clock. Reisewagen seit fünf Uhr früh.
God, what a piece of flesh! Recht ein gestelltes Ding!
(*to Octavian*)
Do not run away. Bleib' Sie [da] hier, mein Herz.
I've something more to tell you. Ich hab' Ihr was zu sagen.
(*to the Marschallin, aloud*)
All my servants are here, huntsmen and Meine ganze Livree, Stallpagen, Jäger,
  grooms and footmen— alles—
(*eating voraciously*)
They are all gathered in the courtyard with Alles unten im Hof zusammt meinem
  my almoner. Almosenier.

MARSCHALLIN
(*to Octavian*)

You may go. Geh' Sie nur.

BARON
(*to Octavian*)

Give me another biscuit. Stay a while. Hat Sie noch ein Biskoterl? Bleib' Sie doch!
(*aside*)
You are the sweetest angel, child, a proper Sie ist ein süsser Engelsschatz, ein sauberer.
  pet.
(*to the Marschallin*)
We're on our way to the "White Horse Inn" Sind auf dem Weg zum "Weissen Ross" wo
  where I shall be staying till tomorrow wir logieren, heisst bis übermorgen—
  morning—
(*aside to Octavian*)
I'll stick at no expense if we— Ich gäb' was Schönes drum, mit Ihr—
(*to the Marschallin, very loud*)
—tomorrow morning— —bis übermorgen—
(*quickly to Octavian*)
Just you and I all alone together: unter vier Augen zu scharmutzieren!
  Ah! Wie?
(*The Marschallin laughs at Octavian's impudent playacting.*)

BARON
(*to the Marschallin*)

Then we're invited to stay with Faninal. Dann zieh'n wir ins Palais von Faninal.
Beforehand I have to choose a fitting Natürlich muss ich vorher den
  ambassador— Bräutigamsaufführer—
(*angrily to Octavian*)
Will you wait a minute?— Will Sie denn nicht warten?—
To my well-endowed and lovely bride I will an die wohlgeborne Jungfer Braut deputieren
  send him,
With the silver rose in his hand der die silber[ne] Rosen überbringt
As the old custom is among noblemen. nach der hochadeligen Gepflogenheit.

MARSCHALLIN

On whom of all our kinsfolk has Your Lordship's choice fallen To act as his ambassador?	Und wen von der Verwandtschaft haben Euer Liebden für dieses Ehrenamt ausgerseh'n?

BARON

It is only because I need Your Highness' counsel on this question That I have made so bold to come so early and to appear all travel-stained—	Die Begierde, darüber Euer Gnaden Ratschlag einzuholen, hat mich so kühn gemacht, in Reisekleidern bei Dero heutigem Lever—

MARSCHALLIN

You wish?	Von mir?

BARON

To beg humbly the favour that I asked for in my letter. I hope I don't presume too much, that with my request I have given offense to you—	Gemäss brieflich in aller Devotion getaner Bitte. Ich bin doch nicht so unglücklich mit dieser devotesten Supplik Dero Missfallen—

(leaning back, to Octavian)

You could do with me anything you wanted. You're just the one for me!	Sie könnte mit mir machen, was Sie wollte. Sie hat das Zeug dazu!

MARSCHALLIN

How so, of course not. We must find someone To be ambassador and call upon your bride, One of our kinsfolk—whom to choose? Our cousin Preysing? Well! Or cousin Lamberg? I wonder—	Wie denn, natürlich! Einen Aufführer für Euer Liebden ersten Bräutigamsbesuch aus der Verwandtschaft—wen denn nur? den Vetter Preysing? Wie? Den Vetter Lamberg? Ich werde—

BARON

I leave it to Your Highness's absolute discretion.	Dies liegt in Euer Gnaden allerschönsten Händen.

MARSCHALLIN

'Tis well. Will you not come to supper, then, dear Cousin? Let's say tomorrow, will you? I'll be prepared with suggestions.	Ganz gut. Will Er mit mir zu Abendessen, Vetter? Sagen wir morgen, will Er? Dann proponier' ich Ihm einen.

BARON

For such grace and kindness I thank Your Highness.	Euer Gnaden sind die Herablassung selber.

MARSCHALLIN
(rising)

And now...	Indess...

BARON
(aside)

You must come back again. I'll stay until you do.	Dass Sie mir wiederkommt! Ich geh' nicht eher fort!

MARSCHALLIN
(to herself)

Oho!	Oho!

(aloud)

Stay where you are! And is that all now You wish to ask of me?	Bleib' Sie nur da! Kann ich dem Vetter für jetzt noch dienlich sein?

BARON

I hesitate to ask, But I'd be grateful to have an introduction To your attorney If I may. I need advice on my marriage deed.	Ich schäme mich bereits: An Euer Gnaden Notari eine Recommandation wäre mir lieb. Es handelt sich um den Eh'vertrag.

MARSCHALLIN

My attorney is coming this morning. Go to see, Mariandl, If by chance he's in the anteroom and waiting.	Mein Notari kommt öfters des Morgens. Schau Sie doch Mariandl, ob er nicht in der Antichambre ist und wartet.

58

BARON

Why send the girl away?	Wozu das Kammerzofel?
She really ought to be here and at your service.	Euer Gnaden beraubt sich der Bedienung
I'll not allow it.	um meinetwillen!

(*He holds her back.*)

MARSCHALLIN

| Let her be, Cousin, so that she may go. | Lass Er doch, Vetter, sie mag ruhig geh'n. |

BARON
(*eagerly*)

Oh, I can't agree. Stay here now beside her Ladyship.	Das geb' ich nicht zu! Bleib' Sie [da] hier zu Ihrer Gnaden Wink.
'Twill not be long before a footman comes.	Es kommt gleich wer von der Livree herein!
Can't let her go unprotected, bless my soul,	Ich liess' ein solches Goldkind, meiner Seel',
Why, God knows what my lackeys might do to her.	nicht unter das infame Lakaienvolk!

(*carressing Octavian*)

MARSCHALLIN

| But Your Lordship is much too concerned. | Euer Liebden sind allzu besorgt. |

(*Enter the Major-Domo.*)

BARON

| Ah, here he is, you see! | Da! hab' ich's nicht gesagt? |
| He's come here no doubt with a message for you. | Er wird Euer Gnaden [was] zu melden haben. |

MARSCHALLIN
(*to the Major-Domo*)

| Struhan, tell me, is my attorney in the anteroom waiting? | Struhan, hab' ich meinen Notari in der Vorkammer warten? |

MAJOR-DOMO

Yes, the attorney's waiting there, Your Highness,	Fürstliche Gnaden haben den Notari,
Likewise the steward, and likewise the chef,	dann den Verwalter, dann den Kuchelchef,
Then there's an alleged singer with his flute	dann von Excellenz Silva hergeschickt
As well, sent here by the Count Silva.	ein Sänger mit einen Flötisten.

(*drily*)

| Of course all the customary riffraff. | Ansonsten das gewöhnliche Bagagi. |

BARON
(*pushes his chair behind the Major-Domo's back, and tenderly takes the hand of the supposed chamber-maid; to Octavian*)

Say, have you ever	Hat Sie schon einmal
Been with a cavalier in tête-à-tête	mit einem Kavalier im tête-à-tête
Together at supper?	zu Abend gegessen?

(*Octavian simulates embarrassment.*)

BARON

| No? I bet your eyes'll open. Will you? | Nein? Da wird Sie Augen machen. Will Sie? |

OCTAVIAN
(*softly, in confusion*)

| I don't really know if I ought. | I' weiss halt nit, ob i dös derf. |

(*The Marschallin observes the pair as she listens attentively to the Major-Domo, and cannot refrain from laughing. The Major-Domo bows and retires, thus exposing the two to the Marschallin's view.*)

MARSCHALLIN
(*laughing, to the Major-Domo*)

| Let them wait there. | Warten lassen. |

(*Exit Major-Domo; the Baron tries to appear at his ease, and assumes a serious air.*)

MARSCHALLIN
(*laughing*)

| My cousin is, I notice, not too particular. | Der Vetter ist, ich seh' es, kein Kostverächter. |

With you, Your Highness,	Mit Euer Gnaden

(breathing more freely)

One is quite at ease. There's no silly prudery and devout pretences,	ist man frei daran. Da gibt's keine Flausen, keine Etiquette;
And no insistence on etiquette.	keine spanische Tuerei!

(He kisses the Marschallin's hand)

MARSCHALLIN
(amused)

Even when you have a bride to be?	Aber wo Er doch ein Bräutigam ist?

BARON
(half rising, leaning towards her) [17]

Is that any reason to live like a monk?	Macht das einen lahmen Esel aus mir?
For am I not like a hunting hound always pursuing quarry	Bin ich da nicht wie ein guter Hund auf einer guten Fährte?
And very hot on every scent, to left or right?	Und doppelt scharf auf jedes Wild: nach links, nach rechts?

MARSCHALLIN

I see it is for you a profession to follow the chase.	Ich seh', Euer Liebden betreiben es als Profession.

BARON

That is my pleasure.	Das will ich meinen.
For the chase I know nothing to suit me better.	Wüsste nicht, welche mir besser behagen könnte.
Your Highness, I must commiserate with You, that you only know—just what shall I say—	Ich muss Euer Gnaden sehr bedauern, dass Euer Gnaden nur—wie drück' ich mich aus—
Only know the feelings of one defending her virtue.	die verteidigenden Erfahrungen besitzen.
Parole d'honneur! But they're not in the least like the feelings that men know.	Parole d'honneur! Es geht nichts über die von der anderen Seite!

MARSCHALLIN
(laughing)

I doubt it not, variety is the spice of life.	Ich glaub' Ihm, dass die sehr mannigfaltig sind.

BARON

In the whole of the year, in the whole of the day, there is never—	So viel Zeiten hat das Jahr, so viel Stunden der Tag, da ist keine—

MARSCHALLIN

Never?	Keine?

BARON

A time—	Wo nicht—

MARSCHALLIN

A time?	Wo nicht?

BARON

A time in which little Cupid Will not grant a favour to us men.	Wo nicht dem Knaben Cupido ein Geschenkerl abzulisten wär'!
So we men are no roosters and no stags,	Dafür ist man kein Auerhahn und kein Hirsch,
Rather we are Lords of Creation,	sondern ist man Herr der Schöpfung,
Nor are we ruled by the moon like you women, begging your pardon!	dass man nicht dem Kalender forciert ist, halten zu Gnaden!
For example, in May it is just right for lover's delights	Zum Exempel der Mai ist recht lieb für's verliebte Geschäft,
(You ask any child)	dass weiss jedes Kind,
But of course I say	aber ich sage:
Better in August, June or July.	Schöner ist Juni, Juli, August.
We have nights then.	Da hat's Nächte!
To us at home in summer comes an army Of girls from Bohemia; in a swarm they cross the border:	Da ist bei uns da droben so ein Zuzug von jungen Mägden aus dem Böhmischen herüber:
And it's pleasant sometimes to induce	ihrer zwei, dreie halt ich oft

Just two or three to stay with me	bis im November mir im Haus.
Till the autumn falls.	Dan erst schick' ich sie heim!
They come at harvest time, nor do they refuse to work, whatever the task.	Zur Ernte kommen sie und sind auch ansonsten anstellig und gut,

(chuckling)

When 'tis done, they go home.—	dann erst schick' ich sie heim.—
And how they agree,	Und wie sich das mischt,
The active, lissom folk of Bohemia, sad and sweet,—	das junge, runde böhmische Völkel schwer und süss,
With those of our land, of true German stock,	mit denen im Wald und denen im Stall,
So different, sharp and sour	dem Deutschen Schlag scharf und herb
Like a northern wine—	wie ein Retzer Wein—
Yet they agree so well!	wie sich das mischen tut!
And everywhere lovers are waiting and seeking each other,	Und überall steht was und lauert und schielt durch den Gattern,
And whispering sweet nothings in tenderest accents,	und schleicht zu einander und liegt bei einander,
And everywhere all day	und überall singt was,
And night joyfully singing	und schupft sich in den Hüften,
And milking	und melkt was
And reaping	und mäht was
With a will, and dabbling in the burns and the village pond.	und plantscht und plätschtert was im Bach und in der Pferdeschwemm.

MARSCHALLIN
(much diverted)

And you are everywhere keeping a watch?	Und Er ist überall dahinter her?

BARON

Would I could be, like Jupiter, happy in a thousand disguises!	Wollt, ich könnt sein wie Jupiter selig in tausend Gestalten!
I could use the whole thousand.	Wäre Verwendung für jede!

MARSCHALLIN

What, even the bull? So crude would you be?	Wie, auch für den Stier? So grob will Er sein?
You should ride as a cloud in heaven and go sailing o'er the mountains	Oder möchte er die Wolken spielen und daher gesäuselt kommen
Like a scented summer breeze.	als ein Streiferl nasse Luft?

BARON
(very gaily)

That depends, yes, it depends.	Je nachdem, all's je nachdem.
For women, look you, must be wheedled and captured in a thousand different ways.	Das Frauenzimmer hat gar vielerlei Arten, wie es will genommen sein.
For one is all humble and shy.	Da ist die demütige Magd.
The next, a limb of the Devil, straight from Hell,	Und da die trotzige Teufelskreatur,
Clouts you and beats your brains out with a broomstick.	haut dir die schwere Stalltür an den Schädel—
Then the third, who giggling and sobbing will lose her head—	Und da ist, die kichernd und schluchzend den Kopf verliert,
That one I like—	die hab' ich gern,
And then another—look in her eyes—there's a devil, cold and repelling,	und jener wieder, der sitzt im Auge ein kalter, rechnender Satan.
Bide but your time—sure 'twill come—	Aber es kommt eine Stunde,
You'll discover how that devil is yielding	da flackert dieses lauernde Auge
And relenting.	und der Satan,
And when his last venomous glances he darts at me	indem er ersterbende Blicke dazwischen schiesst,

(with gusto)

That flavours the banquet past believing.	der würzt mir die Mahlzeit unvergleichlich.

MARSCHALLIN

'Tis you that's a devil, on my soul!	Er selber ist eine, meiner Seel'!

BARON

Yet another—pray give me leave— whom no-one will look at:	Und wär' eine—haben die Gnad'—die keiner anschaut:

61

In tatters and rags she slinks along,	Im schmutzigen Kittel schlumpt sie her,
Crouches 'mid ashes by the hearth—	hockt in der Aschen hinterm Herd—
She, if the right hour have but struck for your wooing,	die, wo du sie angehst zum richtigen Stündl
She's not wanting!	die hat's in sich!
A wild amazement—	Ein solches Staunen—
Stunned and bewildered, halting	gar nicht begreifen können
'Twixt fear and shame;	und Angst und Scham;
At last she yields, like one distraught with excess of joy,	und auf die letzt so eine rasende Seligkeit,
To think that he,	dass sich der Herr,
The master and lord	der gnädige Herr
So far descends to look upon her lowliness!	herabgelassen gar zu ihrer Niedrigkeit!

MARSCHALLIN

| You know more than your A-B-C. | Er weiss mehr als das A-B-C. |

BARON

Then there are others who want to be caught by stealth,	Da gibt es welche, die wollen beschlichen sein,
Soft as the wind a-blowing through the fresh cut hay.	sanft, wie der Wind das frisch-gemähte Heu beschleicht.
The best one, by Gad,	Und welche—da gilt's,

(*to Octavian, who has put the tray back on the breakfast table, and during the foregoing come up close on the Baron's left in amusement*)

Like a tiger you jump on her back,	Wie ein Luchs hinterm Rücken heran
Kick the milk-stool away,	und den Melkstuhl gepackt,
Then she lies there defenceless.	dass sie taumelt und hinschlägt!

(*chuckling complacently*)

| Let there be hay stacked for comfort close at hand. | Muss halt ein Heu in der Nähe dabei sein. |

(*Octavian bursts out laughing.*)

MARSCHALLIN

| Ha! What a man! What victories! | Nein! Er agiert mir gar zu gut! |
| Let go the child, I say. | Lass Er mir doch das Kind! |

BARON

(*to Octavian, without embarrassment*)

Meanest of attics can never disarm me,	Weiss mich ins engste Versteck zu bequemen,
Splendour of boudoir can never alarm me.	weiss in Alkoven galant mich zu [be]nehmen.
Fain would I clothe me in scores of disguises,	Hätte Verwendung für tausend Gestalten
For as many enterprises.	tausend Jungfern festzuhalten.
None comes amiss whether simple or cunning,	Wäre mir keine zu junge, zu herbe,
Luring me on, or my company shunning,	keine zu niedrige, keine zu derbe!
Splendour of boudoir can never alarm me,	Tät mich für keinem Versteck nicht schämen,
All are for me, naught can disarm me.	seh' ich was Lieb's: ich muss mir's nehmen.

OCTAVIAN

(*instantly playing his role again*)

No, I won't go courtin' with you,	Na, zu dem Herrn, da ging i net,
I do not think it right,	da hätt' i an Respect,
Mercy, what would my mother say!	na was mir da passieren könnt,
Sure I should die of fright.	da wär i gar zu g'schreckt.
I don't know what you say,	I wass net, was er meint,
I don't know why I should.	i wass net, was er will.
One thing I know is, 'tis for no good,	Aber was z'viel is, das ist zuviel.
Mercy! What would my mother say!	Na was mir da passieren könnt,
I'd be too scared for funning,	Das is ja net zum sagen,
You look too bold and cunning,	zu so an Herrn da ging i net,
I'd be too scared for funning.	mir tat's die Red' verschlagen.
Such sport leads many a poor girl to her ruin!	Da tät sich unsereins mutwillig schaden:

62

I'm frightened, Your Highness, look what he's doin'.	I hab' so an Angst vor ihm, fürstliche Gnaden.

MARSCHALLIN

Ha! What a man! What victories!	Nein, Er agiert mir gar zu gut!
Ha! What a hero! Ha! What a hero!	Er ist ein Rechter! Er ist der Wahre!
Let that child be, I say.	Lass Er mir doch das Kind!
But of every hundred I see each day,	Er ist ganz, was die andern dreiviertel sind.
There are ninety like him, 'tis still the same story,	Wie ich Ihn so seh', so seh' ich hübsch viele.
They find there's one glory, in all that's unseemly!	Das sind halt die Spiele, die euch convenieren!
And we, Heaven knows,—we feel all the sorrow,	Und wir, Herr Gott! Wir leiden den Schaden,
We bear the hard blows,	wir leiden den Spott,
But perchance women sin more deeply than men.	und wir haben's halt auch net anders verdient.
What manners are those!	Und jetzt sakerlott,

(with feigned severity)

Now let the child be!	jetzt lass Er das Kind!

BARON

(letting go of Octavian and assuming a dignified manner again)

Pray will Your Highness give me the hussy there To come to my intended bride as her servant?	Geben mir Euer Gnaden den Grassaff' da zu meiner künftigen Frau Gemahlin Bedienung.

MARSCHALLIN

What? my favourite? Tell me what for?	Wie, meine Kleine da? Was sollte die?
I'm sure your bride will have no need of her.	Die Fräulein Braut wird schon versehen sein
Such a choice she would wish to make unaided.	und nicht ansteh'n auf Euer Liebden Auswahl.

BARON

I never saw such a promising wench.	Das ist ein feines Ding! Kreuzsakerlott!
She has a drop of good blood in her.	Da ist ein Tropfen gutes Bluts dabei!

OCTAVIAN

(aside)

A drop of good blood!	Ein Tropfen gutes Bluts!

MARSCHALLIN

But Your Lordship is really most observant!	Euer Liebden haben ein scharfes Auge!

BARON

Of course.	Geziemt sich.

(confidentially)

I think it important that we persons of noble Birth and breeding should look for noble blood in all our servants.	Find' in der Ordnung, dass Personen von Stand in solcher Weise von adeligem Blut bedient werden.
I have one here who's a bastard of mine.	Führ' selbst ein Kind meiner Laune mit mir.

OCTAVIAN

(still listening with much amusement, aside)

He's brought his own bastard?	Ein Kind seiner Laune?

MARSCHALLIN

What? And a girl too? I certainly hope not!	Wie? Gar ein Mädel? Das will ich nicht hoffen!

BARON

(emphatically)

No, 'tis a son—with all the Lerchenau features in his face.	Nein, einen Sohn. Trägt lerchenauisches Gepräge im Gesicht.

MARSCHALLIN

'Tis a son!	Einen Sohn!

BARON

He is my body servant.	Halt' ihn als Leiblakai.

MARSCHALLIN
(laughing)

| His bodyservant! | Als Leiblakai! |

OCTAVIAN

| His bodyservant! | Als Leiblakai! |

BARON

So if Your Highness should presently order	Wenn Euer Gnaden dann werden befehlen,
Me to deliver the silver rose to your hands,	dass ich die silberne Rosen darf Dero Händen übergeben,
'Tis my son who will be the one who will bring it.	wird er es sein, der sie herauf bringt.

MARSCHALLIN

| I understand. But a moment I beg. | Sol mich recht freuen. Aber wart Er einmal. |

(making a sign to Octavian)

| Mariandel! | Mariandel! |

BARON

| Please will Your Highness give me this hussy? I really need her! | Geben mir Euer Gnaden das Zofel! Ich lass nicht locker. |

MARSCHALLIN

| Ah! Go and bring the miniature gold medallion. | Ei! Geh Sie [nur] und bring Sie das Medaillon her. |

OCTAVIAN
(softly)

| Therese, Therese, beware. | Theres'! Theres', gib acht! |

MARSCHALLIN
(as before)

| Bring it quick. I know very well what I do. | Bring's nur schnell! Ich weiss schon, was ich tu'. |

BARON
(looking after Octavian)

| Gad, should be a young princess. | [15] Könnt eine junge Fürstin sein. |

(conversationally)

I've planned for my bride that I would order a copy	Hab' vor, meiner Braut eine getreue Kopie
Of my pedigree as a wedding gift.	meines Stammbaums zu spendieren—
Also a lock of the first Lord Lerchenau a devout supporter of the church	nebst einer Lokke vom Ahnherrn Lerchenau, der ein grosser Klosterstifter war
And also a Lord Lieutenant and Governor Of the Carinthian March.	und Obersterblandhofmeister in Kärnten und in der windischen Mark.

(Octavian brings the miniature from the bed alcove.)

MARSCHALLIN

| Would Your Lordship care to have this gallant gentleman | Wollen Euer Gnaden leicht den jungern Herrn da |
| To take the silver rose to your lady? | als Bräutigamsaufführer haben? |

BARON
(in light conversational tones)

| Without a glance I trust Your Highness. | Bin ungeschauter einverstanden! |

MARSCHALLIN
(with slight hesitation)

| It's my young cousin, the Count Octavian. | Mein junger Vetter, der Graf Octavian. |

BARON
(still very courteously)

| Who could wish a more distinguished envoy? | Wüsste keinen vornehmeren zu wünchen! |
| I shall be obliged beyond all words to His Lordship. | Wär in Devotion dem jungen Herrn sehr verbunden! |

MARSCHALLIN
(quickly)

| Look at him well! | Seh' Er ihn an! |

(She holds the miniature towards him.)

BARON
(looking first at the miniature, then at the maid)

| How like they are! | Die Ähnlichkeit! |

MARSCHALLIN	
Yes, yes.	Ja, ja.
BARON	
It's the very spitting image.	[Wie] Aus dem Gesicht geschnitten!
MARSCHALLIN	
It has caused me myself some surprise.	Hab' mir auch schon Gedanken gemacht.
(pointing to the miniature)	
Rofrano, the younger brother of the Marquis.	Rofrano, des Herrn Marchese zweiter Bruder.
BARON	
Octavian Rofrano! 'Tis no light thing, coming of such a house	Octavian Rofrano! Da ist man wer, wenn man aus solchem Haus,
(pointing to the maid)	
And even though it's by the kitchen door.	und wärs auch bei der Domestikentür!
MARSCHALLIN	
That is why I prefer her over all the rest.	Darum halt ich sie auch wie was Besonderes.
BARON	
Most fitting.	Geziemt sich.
MARSCHALLIN	
Always in waiting on me.	Immer um meine Person.
BARON	
Quite right.	Sehr wohl.
MARSCHALLIN	
But get you gone now, Mariandel, off you go.	Jetzt aber geh' Sie, Mariandel, mach' Sie fort.
BARON	
What's that? She's coming back though?	Wie denn? Sie kommt doch wieder?
MARSCHALLIN	
(intentionally ignoring the Baron)	
Admit all who are there waiting outside.	Und lass Sie die Antichambre herein.
(Octavian goes towards the folding door on the right.)	
BARON	
(following him)	
Most lovely child!	Mein schönstes Kind!
OCTAVIAN	
(by the door on the right)	
You can come in now!	Derft's eina geh'!
(running to the other door)	
BARON	
(following him)	
I am your humble servant. Let me have a word with you alone.	Ich bin Ihr Serviteur! Geb'Sie doch einen Augenblick Audienz!
OCTAVIAN	
(slamming the little door in the Baron's face)	
Be back soon.	I komm glei.

(At this moment an old tirewoman enters through the same door. The Baron retreats disappointed. Two footmen come from the left and bring a screen from the alcove. The Marschallin retires behind the screen, the tirewoman following her. The dressing-table is brought to the centre of the stage. Footmen open the folding door on the left. Enter the Notary, the Head-cook, followed by a scullion carrying the Menu Book. Then the Milliner, a Scholar with a huge tome, and the Animal Seller with tiny dogs and an ape. Valzacchi and Annina slipping in quickly behind these, take the foremost place on the left. The Noble Widow with her three daughters take places on the right; all are in deep mourning. The Major-domo leads the Singer and the Flute Player to the front. The Baron, in the background, makes a sign to a footman, gives him an order, and points, "Here, through the back door".)

THREE NOBLE ORPHANS	
(shrilly)	
Three poor but noble little orphans–	Drei arme adelige Waisen–

(The Noble Widow signals to them not to shriek so, and to kneel down.)

THREE ORPHANS
(*kneeling*)

Three poor but noble little orphans	Drei arme adelige Waisen
Lie weeping at your Highness' feet.	erflehen Dero hohen Schutz!

MILLINER
(*loudly*)

Le Chapeau Paméla! La poudre à la reine de Golconde!	Le Chapeau Paméla! La poudre à la reine de Golconde!

ANIMAL SELLER

Pretty monkeys to tease your flunkeys,	Schöne Affen, wenn Durchlaut schaffen
Bright parakeets and birds from Africa.	auch Vögel hab ich da, aus Afrika.

THREE ORPHANS

Our father in youth died a glorious death for his country,	Der Vater ist jung auf dem Felde der Ehre gefallen,
It is out fondest wish to do the same as he.	ihm dieses nachzutun ist unser Herzensziel.

MILLINER

Le chapeau Paméla! C'est la merveille du monde!	Le chapeau Paméla! C'est la merveille du monde!

ANIMAL SELLER

Cockatoo and painted jay.	Papageien hätt' ich da,
From India and Africa.	aus Indien und Afrika.
Puppies quite small,	Hunderln, so klein
House-trained and all, there's no mess at all.	und schon zimmerrein.

(*The Marschallin steps out, all bow low. The Baron has come forward on the left.*)

MARSCHALLIN
(*to the Baron*)

I now present to you, dear Cousin, my man of law.	Ich präsentier' Euer Liebeden hier den Notar.

(*The Notary, bowing towards the dressing-table at which the Marschallin has seated herself, steps towards the Baron on the left. The Marschallin summons the youngest of the three orphans to her side, takes a purse from the Majordomo, gives it to the girl, and kisses her on the forehead. The Scholar tries to come forward and offer the Marschallin his book. Valzacchi darts in front of him and pushes him aside.*)

VALZACCHI
(*flourishing a black-edged news-sheet*)[18]

The scandal newspaper, Your Highness!	Die swarze Seitung! Fürstlike Gnade!
All the latest news and scandal!	Alles 'ier ge'eim gesrieben!
Only given to famous people,	Nur für 'ohe Persönlikeite
The secret gossip.	Die swarze Seitung!
There's a dead man in the anteroom of	Eine Leikname in 'Interkammer
One of the ministers of state!	von eine gräflike Palais!
And a doctor's wife helping her lover	Eine Bürgersfrau mit der amante
To poison the husband	vergiften den Hehemann,
Last night at three o'clock.	diese Nackt um dreie Huhr!

MARSCHALLIN

Take your tales to the kitchen door!	Lass er mich mit dem Tratsch in Ruh!

VALZACCHI

But Lady,	In Gnaden!
Tutte Quante are as true as de Bible	tutte quante Vertraulikeite
From de great big world.	aus die grosse Welt!

MARSCHALLIN

I will not listen! Take your tales to the kitchen door.	Ich will nix wissen! Lass er mich mit dem Tratsch in Ruh'!

(*Valzacchi retreats with a regretful bow.*)

THREE ORPHANS
(*They have all and, finally, their Mother kissed the Marschallin's hand, and are ready to leave.*)

(*in a whining tone*)

Joy and blessing, all confessing,	Glück und Segen allerwegen Euer Gnaden
lift their voices in your praise.	hohem Sinn!

| We shall count the high-born bounty of Your Highness all our days. | Eingegraben steht erhaben er in unserm Herzen drin! |

(Exeunt with their Mother.)

(The Hairdresser enters hastily, his Assistant rushing after him with coat-tails flying. The Hairdresser carefully scans the Marschallin; looks solemn; retreats. He is examining her looks today. In the meantime the Assistant at the dressing-table is unpacking. The Hairdresser pushes several people back so as to have more room. After a little consideration he forms his plan, bustles up to the Marschallin with decision, and begins to do her hair. Enter a footman in pink, black, and silver bearing a note. The Major-domo is at his hand with a silver salver, on which he presents it to the Marschallin. The Hairdresser stands back to allow her to read it. His Assistant hands him new tongs. The Hairdresser waves them to and fro to cool them. After a questioning glance at the Marschallin, who nods, the Assistant hands him the note. He smiles, and uses it to cool the tongs.
Meanwhile the Singer has taken up his position holding his music. The Flute-Player accompanies him, watching him over his shoulder. The Servants are at the front on the right, the others stand in the background.)

SINGER

Di rigori armato il seno	[19] Di rigori armato il seno
Contro amor mi ribellai	Contro amor mi ribellai
Ma fui vinto in un baleno	Ma fui vinto in un baleno
In mirar due vaghi rai.	In mirar due vaghi rai.
Ahi! che resiste puoco	Ahi! che resiste puoco
Cor di gelo a stral di fuoco.	Cor di gelo a stral di fuoco.

(The Hairdresser hands the curling tongs to his Assistant and applauds the singer. Then he proceeds with arranging the Marschallin's curls. In the meantime a footman has admitted the Baron's body-servant, almoner and huntsman by the small door.
It is a strange trio. The body-servant is a tall young fellow with a foolish, insolent expression. He carries a jewel-case of red morocco under his arm. The almoner is an unkempt village priest, four feet high, but a strong and impudent-looking imp. The huntsman looks as if he had been carting dung before he was pushed into his ill-fitting livery. The almoner and the body-servant seem to be fighting for precedence, and trip each other up. They steer a course to the left, towards their Master, in whose vicinity they come to a halt.)

BARON
(seated on the armchair at the front on the left, to the Notary who is standing in front of him taking instructions. In an undertone)

As first instalment, quite as a separate gift,	Als Morgengabe–ganz separatim jedoch–
Before the dowry, you understand me, do you not?–	und vor der Mitgift–bin ich verstanden, Herr Notar?–
The house and lands of Gaunersdorf return to me!	kehrt Schloss und Herrschaft Gaunersdorf an mich zurück!
Redeemed of debt and with manorial rights undiminished	Von Lasten frei und ungemindert an Privilegien
Just as my father held them for his whole life long.	so wie mein Vater selig sie besessen hat.

NOTARY
(short of breath)

Your Lordship, it is my painful duty delicately to remind you	Gestatten hochfreiherrliche Gnaden die submisseste Belehrung,
That such a compensation from the wife to the husband,	dass eine Morgengabe wohl vom Gatten an die Gattin,
Instead of from the husband to the wife	nicht aber von der Gattin an den Gatten

(taking a deep breath)

| By contract is not in law or custom possible. | bestellet oder stipuliert zu werden, fähig ist. |

BARON

| That may be so. | Das mag wohl sein. |

NOTARY

| It is so – | Das ist so – |

BARON

| But in a special case – | Aber im besondern Fall – |

NOTARY

The law, Sir, and its wise prescriptions, postulate no special case.	Die Formen und die Praescriptionen kennen keinen Unterschied.

BARON
(shouting)

Then it is time it began to!	Haben ihn aber zu kennen!

NOTARY
(terrified)

Your pardon!	In Gnaden!

BARON
(quietly again, but with insistence, and full of amour-propre)

If one who springs from the very noblest stock should so far condescend	[20] Wenn eines hochadeligen Blutes blühender Spross sich herablässt,
As to take in marriage one almost of the middle classes like Miss Faninal –	im Ehebette einer so gut als bürgerlichen Mamsell Faninal
You understand me?–take her to his bed in fact	—bin ich verstanden?–acte de présence zu machen
Before God and the world, and as one might say,	vor Gott und der Welt, und sozusagen
Under the eye of the Imperial court,	angesichts kaiserlichen Majestät,

(The Flute-Player begins his prelude again.)

Surely, corpo di Bacco! A first instalment	Da wird, corpo di Bacco! Von Morgengabe
Would be only common justice as a sign of thanks	als geziemendem Geschenk dankbarer Devotion
For the sacrifice I am making	für die Hingab' so hohen Blutes
By giving my name to her.	sehr wohl die Rede sein!

(The Singer seems about to begin, but waits for the Baron to be silent.)

NOTARY
(to the Baron in a low voice)

Perhaps, by way of separate conveyance –	Vielleicht, dass man die Sache separatim –

BARON
(in a low voice)

You are a pettifogging fool! As first instalment, I want my house back!	Er ist ein schmählicher Pedant: als Morgengabe will ich das Gütel!

NOTARY
(as before)

Ah, as an especial item in the marriage contract.	Als einen wohl verklausulierten Teil der Mitgift–

BARON
(a little louder)

As first instalment! Will nothing get it through your thick skull?	Als Morgengabe! Geht das [denn] nicht in Seinen Schädel?

NOTARY
(in the same tone)

As a donatio inter vivos or else...	Als eine Schenkung inter vivos oder–

BARON
(banging his fist on the table in a rage, and shouting)

As first instalment!	Als Morgengabe!

SINGER
(during the foregoing discussion)

Ma si caro è'l mio tormento	[19] Ma si caro è'l mio tormento
Dolce è si la piága mia	Dolce è si la piága mia
Ch'il penare è mio contento	Ch'il penare è mio contento
E'l sanarmi è tirannia	E'l sanarmi è tirannia
Ahi! Che resiste puoco–	Ahi! Che resiste puoco–
Cor...	Cor...

(At this point the Baron raises his voice to such a pitch that the Singer breaks off abruptly, as does the Flute Player. The Notary retires to a corner in alarm. The Marschallin summons the Singer and gives him her hand to kiss. The Singer and the Flute Player retire, bowing deeply. The Baron makes as if nothing had happened, waves condescendingly to the Singer, crosses over to his servants, straightens his body servant's tousled hair; then goes to the

small door as if looking for somebody, opens it, peeps out, is annoyed that the chamber-maid is not coming back; snoops about the bed, shakes his head, and comes forward again.)

MARSCHALLIN
(looking at herself in her hand mirror, in an undertone)

My good friend Hippolyte,	Mein lieber Hippolyte,
This will not do, for see how old	heut' haben Sie ein altes Weib aus mir
you've made me look!	gemacht!

(The Hairdresser falls, in consternation, on the Marschallin's coiffure with feverish energy, and changes it again. The Marschallin continues to wear a pensive expression. Valzacchi, followed by Annina, has slunk behind everyone else's backs to the other side of the stage, and now presents himself to the Baron with exaggerated obsequiousness.)

MARSCHALLIN
(to the Major-Domo, over her shoulder)

Tell them all to go!	Abtreten die Leut!

(The Footmen, taking hands, push them all out by the door, which they then close. Only the Scholar, whom the Major-Domo presents to the Marschallin, remains in conversation with her until the close of the episode between Valzacchi, Annina, and the Baron.)

VALZACCHI
(to the Baron)

De Barone needs my help I see,	[21] Ihre Gnade sukt etwas. Ik seh,
De Barone is needing my service.	Ihre Gnade at eine Bedürfnis.
I kann make me useful in all ways.	Ik Kann dienen. Ik kann besorgen.

BARON
(retreating)

And what, Sir, are you, Sir?	Wer ist Er, was weiss Er?

VALZACCHI

De Barone 'e speak out of his eyes	Ihre Gnade Gesikt sprikt ohne Sunge.
Like Italian marble. Come statua di Giove.	Wie ein Hantike: come statua di Giove.

ANNINA

Italian marble ... di Giove ...	Wie eine Hantike ... di Giove ...

BARON

A most remarkable man.	Dass ist ein besserer Mensch.

VALZACCHI

My Lord Barone, we are both your obedient	Erlaukte Gnade, attachieren uns an Sein
servants.	Gefolge.

(falls on his knees, as does Annina)

BARON

You?	Euch?

VALZACCHI, ANNINA

Uncle and niece.	Onkel und Nikte.
Together we do better work.	Su sweien maken alles besser.
Per esempio: De Barone's lady is very	Per esempio: Ihre Gnade at eine junge
young?	Frau—

BARON

And just how do you know, you rascal, you?	Woher weiss Er denn das, Er Teufel Er?

VALZACCHI, ANNINA
(eagerly)

De Barone is a jealous man: dico per dire!	Ihre Gnade ist in Eifersukt: dico per dire!
Now or tomorrow it may be. Affare nostro!	Eut oder Morgen könnte sein. Affare nostro!
Every step de lady may make,	Jede Sritt die Dame sie tut,
Every carriage de lady take,	jede Wagen die Dame steigt,
Every letter de lady may get–	jede Brief die Dame bekommt–
We are there.	wir sind da!
Up de chimney or by de fire, under de	An die Ecke, in die Kamin,' inter die Bette–
carpet–	
Up in de attic or in a cupboard	in eine Schranke, unter die Dache,
In de corner, under de bed –	
We are there.	wir sind da!

(The Marschallin rises. The Hairdresser bows low, and hurries off followed by his Assistant.)

ANNINA

De Barone will not regret it!	Ihre Gnade wird nicht bedauern!

(They hold out their hands for money. He pretends not to notice)

BARON
(in an undertone)

Hm! What a place it is, this old Vienna.   Hm! Was es alles gibt in diesem Wien!
I'll test you now: do you know that girl   Zur Probe nur: kennt Sie die Jungfer
  Mariandel?   Mariandel?

ANNINA
(in an undertone)

Mariandel?   Mariandel?

BARON
(in an undertone)

The serving maid who waits there on Her   Das Zofel hier im Haus bei Ihrer Gnaden?
  Highness?

VALZACCHI
(in a whisper to Annina)

Sai tu? Cosa vuole?   Sai tu? Cosa vuole?

ANNINA
(also whispering)

Niente!   Niente!

VALZACCHI
(to the Baron)

Surely, surely, my niece knows   Sicker! Sicker! Mein Nickte wird
  all about her,   besorgen.
Be assured of that, Your Lordship.   Seien sicker, Ihre Gnade! Wir sind da!
  We are there!

(He holds his hand out again. The Baron ignores him.)

BARON
(leaving the two Italians; to the Marschallin)

May I now introduce   [12] Darf ich das Gegenstück
(discreetly)

The counterpart of your Mariandel   vertraulich zu Dero sauberm Kammerzofel
  to Your Highness?   präsentieren?
(complacently)

I'm told that the likeness is unmistakable.   Die Ähnlichkeit soll, hör ich,
                        unverkennbar sein.

(The Marschallin nods.)

BARON

Leupold, give me the case!   Leupold, das Futterall!

(The young footman presents the case awkardly.)

MARSCHALLIN
(smiling slightly)

He does great honour to his ancestry.   Ich gratulier' Euer Liebden sehr.

BARON
(taking the case from the lad, and signalling to him to retire)

And here I have the silver rose.   Und da ist nun die silberne Rose.
(He is about to open it.) [14]

MARSCHALLIN

Do not disturb it.   Lassen nur drinnen.
Put it down here, please, if you don't mind.   Haben die Gnad' und stellen's dort hin.

BARON

Or shall we call for your Mariandel?   Vielleicht das Zofel soll's übernehmen?
Let me ring.   Ruft man ihr?

MARSCHALLIN

No, let her be. She has her duties too.   Nein lassen nur. Die hat jetzt keine Zeit.
But this I promise, that Count Octavian [6] Doch Sei Er sicher: den Grafen Octavian
  shall be informed.   bitt' ich Ihm auf,
For me he'll consent, I know,   er wird's mir zulieb schon tun
And will duly ride as cavalier   und als Euer Liebden Kavalier
To your bride and present her with   vorfahren mit der Rosen bei der
  the silver rose.   Jungfer Braut.
(indifferently)

70

Leave it there if you will.	Stellen indess nur hin.
And now, dear Cousin, I must say Adieu.	Und jetzt Herr Vetter, sag ich Ihm Adieu.
The time has come for all to leave,	Man retiriert sich jetzt von hier:
Or I shall be too late for church.	Ich werd jetzt in die Kirchen gehn.

(The footmen open the folding doors.)

BARON

Why, Your Highness, it's too much.	Euer Gnaden haben heut
Your kindness and your charm have left me dumb.	durch unversiegte Huld mich tiefst beschämt.

(He makes an obeisance and withdraws ceremoniously. At a signal from him the Notary follows him. His three servants shuffle awkwardly out. The two Italians silently and obsequiously join his train without his noticing them. The footmen close the door. The Major-domo withdraws. The Marschallin is left alone.)

MARSCHALLIN
(alone)

And there he goes, a vain, pretentious pompous fellow,	Da geht er hin, der aufgeblasene schlechte Kerl,
And gets a young and pretty bride and ample dowry as reward.	und kriegt das hübsche junge Ding und einen Pinkel Geld dazu.

(sighing)

He takes it all,	Als müsst's so sein.
And thinks 'tis but his due; and boasts that he greatly honours her!	Und bildet sich noch ein, dass er es ist, der sich was vergibt.
But why trouble myself? The world will have it so.	Was erzürn' ich mich denn? 'sist doch der Lauf der Welt.
I remember a girl, just like this one, [22]	Kann mich auch an ein Mädel erinnern,
Who fresh from the convent was marched	die frisch aus dem Kloster ist in den
Off straight to the holy estate of wedlock.	heiligen Ehestand kommandiert word'n.

(She takes a hand-mirror.)

Where is she now? Ah,	Wo ist die jetzt? Ja,

(sighing)

Go, seek the snows of yesteryear!	such' dir den Schnee vom vergangenen Jahr!
But can it be,	Das sag' ich so:

(quietly)

Can it really be as I say,	Aber wie kann das wirklich sein,
That I was that young girl long ago	dass ich die kleine Resi war
And that I shall one day be called the old Princess ...	und dass ich auch einmal die alte Frau sein werd' ...
The old Princess, the Marshall's old Princess!	Die alte Frau, die alte Marschallin!
"Look now, there goes the old Princess Theresa!"	"Siegst es, da geht's, die alte Fürstin Resi!"
How can this come to pass?	Wie kann denn das geschehen?
Is this indeed the will of God?	Wie macht denn das der liebe Gott?
For I am still I, the very same.	Wo ich doch immer die gleiche bin.
But if indeed it must be so,	Und wenn er's schon so machen muss,
Why then must I sit here looking on,	warum lässt er mich denn zuschau'n dabei
And see it all, so clear? Why are these things not hid from me?	mit gar so klarem Sinn? Warum versteckt er's nicht vor mir?
This all is mystery, all mystery,	Das alles ist geheim, so viel geheim,
And we are here on earth	Und man ist dazu da,

(sighing)

To bear it all.	[5] dass man's erträgt.
But to know "how?"–	Und in den "Wie"

(very quietly)

In that lies all the difference–	da liegt der ganze Unterschied–

(to Octavian who enters from the right in riding-dress and riding-boots; calmly, half smiling)

Ah! You are back again?	Ach, Du bist wieder da!

OCTAVIAN
(tenderly)

You're lost in sadness.	Und Du bist traurig!

MARSCHALLIN

The mood has flown again. You know me, how I am.	Es ist ja schon vorbei. Du weisst ja, wie ich bin.
One moment merry, one moment weeping.	Ein halb Mal lustig, ein halb Mal traurig.
My thoughts, I cannot command them, I know not how.	Ich kann halt meinen Gedanken nicht kommandier'n.

OCTAVIAN

I know why you have been in tears, my heart.	Ich weiss, warum Du traurig bist, Mein Schatz.
You were beside yourself and panic-stricken.	Weil Du erschrocken bist und Angst gehabt hast.
Am I not right? Confess to me:	Hab' ich nicht recht? Gesteh' mir nur:
You were terrified,	Du hast Angst gehabt,
My angel, my loved one	Du Süsse, Du Liebe,
For me, for me!	Um mich, um mich!

MARSCHALLIN

A little perhaps,	Ein bissel vielleicht,
But I recovered my courage and to myself I said: now what indeed should I fear.	aber ich hab' mich erfangen und hab' mir vorgesagt: Es wird schon nicht dafür steh'n.
And does it really matter?	Und wär's dafür gestanden?

OCTAVIAN
(*gaily*)

It was not the Feldermarschall,	Und es war kein Feldmarschall,
But a silly clown, your cousin, and you are all mine,	nur ein spassiger Herr Vetter und Du gehörst mir,
You are all mine.	Du gehörst mir!

MARSCHALLIN
(*pushing him aside*)

Dearest, embrace me not so much.	Taverl, umarm' Er nicht zu viel.
Who tries to hold too much, holds nothing fast.	Wer allzuviel umarmt, der hält nichts fest.

OCTAVIAN
(*passionately*)

Say you are mine alone, mine!	Sag', dass Du mir gehörst! Mir!

MARSCHALLIN

Oh! Do but be good, be tender and gentle and kind and wise.	Oh, sei Er jetzt sanft, sei Er gescheit und sanft und gut.

(*Octavian is about to answer excitedly.*)

I beg you now, do not be like all the others are.	Nein bitt' schön, sei Er [nur] nicht wie alle Männer sind!

OCTAVIAN
(*starting up suspiciously*)

Like all the others?	Wie alle Männer?

MARSCHALLIN
(*quickly recovering herself*)

Like the Feldmarschall and my cousin Ochs.	Wie der Feldmarschall und der Vetter Ochs.

OCTAVIAN
(*still not satisfied*)

Bichette!	Bichette!

MARSCHALLIN
(*emphatically*)

No, do not be like all the other men.	Sei Er nur nicht, wie all Männer sind.

OCTAVIAN
(*angrily*)

I know nothing of the other men.	Ich weiss nicht, wie alle Männer sind.

(*with sudden tenderness*)

Only I know I love you.	Weiss nur, dass ich Dich lieb hab'.
Bichette, they've taken you away from me.	Bichette, sie haben dich mir ausgetauscht.
Bichette, where have you gone?	Bichette, wo ist sie denn?

MARSCHALLIN
(calmly)

I still am here, my love. Sie ist wohl da, Herr Schatz.

OCTAVIAN

When you are here, then I want to hold you, Ja, ist Sie da? Dann will ich Sie halten,
To protect you from what may befall dass Sie mir nicht wieder entkommt!
(passionately)
And safe by my side clasp you. Packen will ich Sie, packen, dass
Then you will know to whom you belong. Sie es spürt, zu wem Sie gehört–
To me! For I am yours and you are mine! zu mir! Denn ich bin Ihr und Sie ist mein!

MARSCHALLIN
(escaping from him)

Oh, do be good, Quinquin. I feel I know Oh sei Er gut, Quinquin. Mir ist zu Mut,
That all things earthly are but a vanity, dass ich die Schwäche von allem Zeitlichen
  vain, empty dreams; recht spüren muss,
Deep in my heart I know bis in mein Herz hinein,
How we should grasp at naught, wie man nichts halten soll,
How we can cling to naught, wie man nichts packen kann.
How life and its joys slip through Wie alles zerläuft zwischen den Fingern,
  our fingers,
How everything alters if we but grasp it, Wie alles sich auflöst, wonach wir greifen,
Everything fades like shadows, like dreams. alles zergeht wie Dunst und Traum.

OCTAVIAN

Oh God, what do you say? Mein Gott, wie Sie das sagt.
You only want to tell me that you love me Sie will mir doch nur zeigen, dass Sie nicht
  no more. an mir hängt.
(He weeps.)

MARSCHALLIN

Don't be so sad, Quinquin! Sei Er doch gut, Quinquin!
(Octavian weeps more bitterly.)

MARSCHALLIN

Ah, now I am the one who must console Jetzt muss ich noch den Buben dafür
  him, trösten,
For the day, be it soon, be it late, when he Dass er mich über kurz oder lang wird
  will leave me. sitzen lassen.
(She caresses him.)

OCTAVIAN

Be it soon, be it late, Über kurz oder lang?
(angrily)
Who could have put such words into your Wer legt Ihr heut' die Wörter in den Mund,
  mouth, Bichette? Bichette?

MARSCHALLIN

Do my words hurt you so? Dass Ihn das Wort so kränkt!
(Octavian stops his ears.)
The time is coming, Quinquin, Die Zeit im Grunde, Quinquin,
The time, be it sooner or later, what matter. Die Zeit, die ändert doch nichts an den
  Sachen.
For time, how strangely goes its own [23] Die Zeit, die ist ein sonderbar Ding.
  way.
We do not heed it, time has no meaning, Wenn man so hinlebt, ist sie rein gar Nichts.
But there comes a moment when time is Aber dann auf einmal, da spürt man nichts
  all we feel. als sie.
All the world talks of it, all our souls Sie ist um uns herum, sie ist auch in uns
  are filled with it. drinnen.
On every face its mark will show. In den Gesichtern rieselt sie,
Each mirror betrays it, im Spiegel da rieselt sie,
All through my dreams 'tis flowing, in meinem Schläfen fliesst sie.
And now between us two Und zwischen mir und dir
It flows in silence, trickling as in an da fliesst sie wieder, lautlos, wie eine
  hourglass. Sanduhr.
(earnestly)

73

Oh, Quinquin, sometimes I hear it flowing	Oh, Quinquin! Manchmal hör' ich sie fliessen –
Unrelenting.	unaufhaltsam.

(softly)

Sometimes I arise in the dead of night,	Manchmal steh ich auf mitten in der Nacht
Go to my clocks and stop them, every one.	Und lass' die Uhren alle, alle steh'n.
And yet, to be afraid of time is useless.	Allein, man muss sich auch vor ihr nicht fürchten.
For God, mindful of all his children, in his wisdom created it.	Auch sie ist ein Geschöpf des Vaters, der uns alle erschaffen hat.

OCTAVIAN
(tenderly and gently)

My dearest love, why do you torture yourself so with such thoughts?	Mein schöner Schatz, will Sie sich traurig machen mit Gewalt?
Now that I am here,	Wo Sie mich da hat,
And my loving fingers are clasping yours so tenderly,	wo ich meine Finger in Ihre Finger schlinge,
And my eyes look into yours to find an answer,	wo ich mit meinen Augen Ihre Augen suche,
Now that I am here,	Wo Sie mich da hat–
At such a time can you feel like this?	gerade da ist Ihr so zu Mut?

MARSCHALLIN
(very serious)

Quinquin, now or tomorrow, surely,	Quinquin, heut oder morgen geht Er hin
You will go from me, leave me and choose another,	und gibt mich auf, um einer andern willen,

(hesitating a little)

Who's younger and lovelier than I. [14]	die schöner oder junger ist als ich.

OCTAVIAN

So you are trying now to dismiss me	Willst Du mit Worten mich von Dir stossen,
And do with words what your hands refuse?	weil Die die Hände den Dienst nicht tun?

MARSCHALLIN
(calmly)

The day will come unbidden,	Der Tag kommt ganz von selber.
Now or tomorrow it will come, Octavian.	Heut' oder Morgen kommt der Tag, Octavian.

OCTAVIAN

Not now, not tomorrow! I love you so.	Nicht heut', nicht morgen! ich hab' Dich lieb.
Not now nor tomorrow!	Nicht heut', nicht morgen!
The sun shall not rise, that I swear, on such a day!	Wenn's so einen Tag geben muss, i'denk' ihn nicht!
So dreadful a day!	Solch schrecklichen Tag!
That day shall never come,	Ich will den Tag nicht seh'n.
I cannot bear to think of it.	Ich will den Tag nicht denken.
Why break my heart and yours, Therese?	Was quälst Du Dich und mich, Theres'?

MARSCHALLIN

Now or tomorrow, if not tomorrow, very soon.	Heut' oder morgen oder den übernächsten Tag.
I would not torture you, my love.	Nicht quälen will ich Dich, mein Schatz.
'Tis truth I'm speaking, 'tis as true for you as 'tis for me…	Ich sag' was wahr ist, sag's zu mir so gut als [wie] zu Dir.
Let us then lightly meet our fate;	Leicht will ich's machen Dir und mir.
Light must we be,	Leicht muss man sein
With spirits light, with gentle fingers	mit leichtem Herz und leichten Händen
Take all our pleasures, take them and leave them.	halten und nehmen, halten und lassen…
Unless we do much grief awaits us, and God himself won't pity us.	Die nicht so sind, die sträft das Leben und Gott erbarmt sich ihrer nicht.

OCTAVIAN

Today you speak like my confessor.	Sie spricht ja heute wie ein Pater.
Do you tell me that I may never, no,	Soll das heissen, dass ich Sie nie, nie mehr,
Never kiss you and love you till you are faint with rapture?	werd' küssen dürfen, bis Ihr der Atem ausgeht?

(softly)

Quinquin, now you must go. Now you [5,2] Quinquin, Er soll jetzt geh'n, Er soll mich
must leave me; lassen.
I'll go now, go to church, and pray, Ich werd' jetzt in die Kirchen geh'n
And later visit my Uncle Greifenklau, und später fahr' ich zum Onkel Greifenklau,
Who's old and so ailing, der alt und gelähmt ist
And dine with him: 'twill please the und ess' mit ihm: das freut den alten Mann.
dear old man.

This afternoon I will send to your house Und Nachmittag werd' ich Ihm einen
a footman, Lauffer schicken,
Quinquin, and he will tell you Quinquin, und sagen lassen
If I plan to take the air; ob ich in den Prater fahr'.
And if I do Und wenn ich fahr'
And you should wish Und Er hat lust,
You may meet me in the Prater riding so wird Er auch in' [dem] Prater kommen
And you may ride beside my carriage. und neben meinem Wagen reiten.
And now be good. Do as I say. Jetzt sei Er gut und folg' Er mir.

OCTAVIAN
(softly)

As you command, Bichette. Wie Sie befiehlt, Bichette.

(Exit. A pause)

MARSCHALLIN
(Alone. Starting up passionately)

He's gone without even a kiss. Ich hab' Ihn nicht einmal geküsst.

(She rings the bell violently. Footmen hurry in from the right.)

Run and overtake the Count Lauft's dem Herrn Grafen nach
And say that I beg for a word with him. und bitet's ihn noch auf ein Wort herauf.

(The footmen hurry off.)

I have let him go from me, and without Ich hab' ihn fortgeh'n lassen und ihn nicht
a single kiss! einmal geküsst!

(She sits down on the chair by the dressing-table. The footmen return out of breath.)

FIRST FOOTMAN

But the Count is off and away. Der Herr Graf sind auf und davon.

SECOND FOOTMAN

In a flash he seized the bridle. Gleich beim Tor sind aufgesessen.

THIRD FOOTMAN

Swung up in the stirrups. Reitknecht hat gewartet.

FOURTH FOOTMAN

At the door he seized the bridle like the Gleich beim Tor sind aufgesessen wie der
wind. Wind.

FIRST FOOTMAN

Gallopped round the corner like the wind. Waren um die Ecken wie der Wind.

SECOND FOOTMAN

We hurried after. Sind nachgelaufen.

THIRD FOOTMAN

We cried ourselves hoarse. Wir haben geschrien.

FOURTH FOOTMAN

All in vain. War umsonst.

FIRST FOOTMAN

Gallopped round the corner like the wind. Waren um die Ecken wie der Wind.

MARSCHALLIN

Very well. Send Mohamed. Es ist gut, gehts nur wieder.

(The footmen withdraw. The Marschallin calls after them.)

Mohamed please! Den Mohamed!

(The little black boy enters with tinkling bells, as before, and bows.) [9a]

Take this case... Das da trag' ...

Wait till I say where. To Count
  Octavian.
Give it and say,
Within is the silver rose.
He will know what he must do.

[6] Weisst ja nicht wohin. Zum Grafen
  Octavian.
Gib's ab und sag':
Da drinn is die silberne Ros'n.
Der Herr Graf weiss ohnehin.

The Black Boy runs off. The Marschallin leans her head on her hand, and remains deep in thought until the curtain falls. [1]

Ava June as the Marschallin in the ENO production by John Copley. (Photo: Mike Humphrey)

76

Act Two

A room in Herr von Faninal's house. The central doors lead to an antechamber. Doors to right and left. A large window on the right. Chairs against the wall on either side of the main doors. In the rounded corners on either side, are secret doors. A footman stands on either side of the main door. Faninal, Sophie, Marianne Leitmetzerin (her Duenna), the Major-Domo, Footmen. [24, 25, 20, 26]

FANINAL
(on the point of saying good-bye to Sophie)

A solemn day, a festal day,	Ein ernster Tag, ein grosser Tag!
A wondrous day, a sacred day!	Ein Ehrentag, ein heiliger Tag!

(Sophie kisses his hand.)

MARIANNE

The new coach is there with our man on the box.	Der Josef fahrt vor, mit der neuen Kaross',
Its curtains are of sky-blue.	hat himmelblaue Vorhäng',
Four shining horses are there.	vier Apfelschimmel sind dran.

MAJOR-DOMO
(confidentially to Faninal)

It's high time now Your Lordship should be leaving.	Ist höchste Zeit, dass Euer Gnaden fahren.
It's customary for the bride's father	Der hochadelige Bräutigamsvater,
To have taken his	sagt die Schicklichkeit,
Departure from the house	muss ausgefahren sein,
Before the silver Rosenkavalier comes here.	bevor der silberne Rosenkavalier vorfahrt.
It were not seemly	Wär nicht geziemend,
For you to meet him at the palace door.	dass sie sich vor' der Tür begegneten.

(Footmen open the door.)

FANINAL

Heaven help me. When I come again,	In Gottes Namen, Wenn ich wiederkomm',
I shall be leading your bridegroom to be by the hand.	so führ' ich Deinen Herrn Zukünftigen bei der Hand.

MARIANNE

The excellent and noble Baron Lerchenau!	Den edlen und gestrengen Herrn von Lerchenau!

(Exit Faninal. Sophie comes forward alone. Marianne is at the window.)

MARIANNE

Up go the steps. The footmen one by one are springing up behind.	Jetzt steigt er ein. Der Xaver und der Anton springen hinten auf.
The little page has handed up the whip,	Der Stallpag' reicht dem Josef seine Peitsch'n.
And there are faces at every house.	Alle Fenster sind voller Leut'.

SOPHIE

On this most joyful day I praise thee my Maker,	[29] In dieser feierlichen Stunde der Prüfung,
In that Thou dost exalt me high above my worth	Da du mich, o mein Schöpfer, über mein Verdienst erhöhen
And bring me now to thy altar beside the one Thou has willed,	und in den heiligen Ehestand führen willst,

(controlling herself with great difficulty)

And I offer Thee now my heart, my humble heart.	opfer' ich Dir in Demut, mein Herz in Demut auf.
My flesh is too weak to be humble,	Die Demut in mir zu erwecken,
So I must humble myself.	muss ich mich demütigen.

MARIANNE
(very excited)

And half the town is out of doors.	Die halbe Stadt ist auf die Füss'.
See them in the cloister, the good monks one and all are at the windows	Aus dem Seminari schau'n die Hochwüdigen von die Balkoner.
And one old man sits high up upon the roof.	Ein alter Mann sitzt oben auf der Latern'.

(struggling to collect her thoughts)

Humble myself and well remember how guilty, how	Demütigen und recht bedenken: die Sünde, die
Vain, how little worth, how intractable Thy children are!	Schuld, die Niedrigkeit, die Verlassenheit, die Anfechtung!
My mother is dead and I am all alone,	Die Mutter ist tot und ich bin ganz allein.
Here in prayer before Thy throne.	Für mich selbar steh' ich ein.
Here at the altar with thy blessing I stand.	Aber die Ehe ist ein heiliger Stand.

MARIANNE
(as before)

He comes, he comes, with two great coaches.	Er kommt, er kommt in zwei Karossen.
The first one has four horses, it is empty. But the next has six dapple greys.	Die erste ist vierspännig, die ist leer. In der zweiten, sechsspännigen,
I can see him, the Rosenkavalier!	sitzt er selber, der Rosenkavalier.

THREE FOOTMEN
(running before Octavian's carriage in the street below)

Rofrano, Rofrano!	Rofrano, Rofrano!

SOPHIE
(almost losing her self-control)

I will not be swollen with pride of station after marriage – –after my marriage.	Ich will mich niemals meines neuen Standes überheben– –mich überheben.

(She can control herself no longer.)

What is it they cry?	Was rufen denn die?

MARIANNE

They call him the Rosenkavalier and cry the names	Den Namen vom Rosenkavalier und alle Namen
Of all the august relations of your husband, as I hear.	von deiner neuen fürstlich'n [und gräflich'n] Verwandtschaft rufens aus.
Now the servants form a pathway.	Jetzt rangieren sich die Bedienten.
The outriders are beside the door!	Die lakaien springen rückwärts ab!

THREE FOOTMEN
(closer)

Rofrano! Rofrano!	Rofrano! Rofrano!

SOPHIE [2, 26]

Oh, but when my bridegroom comes will everyone	Werden sie mein' Bräutigam sein' Namen
Cry his station, and his name and titles too?	auch so ausrufen, wenn er angefahren kommt!?

THREE FOOTMEN
(right under the window)

Rofrano! Rofrano!	Rofrano! Rofrano!

MARIANNE

The coach door is open and he comes,	Sie reissen den Schlag auf! Er steigt aus!
All in silver clad, he is glittering from head to foot.	Ganz in Silberstück' ist er angelegt, von Kopf zu Fuss.
Like an archangel all on fire.	Wie ein heil'ger Engel schaut er aus.

(She hastily shuts the window.)

SOPHIE

Merciful Heaven!	Herrgott im Himmel!
I know that pride must be a mortal sin.	Ich weiss, der Stolz ist eine schwere Sünd'.
But today never can I humble myself.	Aber jetzt kann ich mich nicht demütigen.
'Tis all in vain.	Jetzt geht's halt nicht!
For my lot is so rare, so rare!	Denn das ist ja so schön, so schön!

Two of Faninal's Footmen quickly open the centre doors. Enter Octavian, bareheaded, dressed all in white and silver, carrying the Silver Rose in his hand. Behind him are his servants in his livery, white and pale green. The Footmen, the Heyducks with their crooked Hungarian swords at their side; the Couriers in white leather with green ostrich plumes. Immediately behind Octavian a black servant carrying his hat, and another Footman who carries the case for the Silver Rose in both hands. Behind these, Faninal's servants. Octavian, taking the rose in his right hand, advances with noble grace towards Sophie; but his youthful features bear traces of embarrassment, and he blushes. Sophie turns deathly pale with excitement at his splendid appearance. They stand facing each other, each disconcerted by the confusion and beauty of the other. [26]

OCTAVIAN
(with slight hesitation)

It is an honour, an enchantment [28]	Mir ist die Ehre widerfahren
To which I'll stay most deeply sensible all my days,	dass ich der hoch - und wohlgeborenen Jungerfer Braut,
To come here as messenger at	in meines Herrn Vetters Namen,
My Cousin Lerchenau's bidding,	dessen zu Lerchenau [Namen],
To offer you as token of his love this rose.	die Rose seiner Liebe überreichen darf.

SOPHIE
(taking the rose)

I am to Your Honour much indebted.	Ich bin Euer Liebden sehr verbunden.
I am to Your Honour to all Eternity indebted.	Ich bin Euer Liebden in aller Ewigkeit verbunden.

(momentary confusion; she smells the rose)

There is a scent in its petals of roses, like the living ones!	Hat einen starken Geruch. Wie Rosen, wie lebendige!

OCTAVIAN

Yes, there's a drop of oil of Persian roses in its heart.	Ja, ist ein Tropfen persischen Rosenöls darein getan.

SOPHIE

Like heavenly, not earthly flowers, like roses	Wie himmlische, nicht irdische, wie Rosen
From golden gardens of Paradise. Think you not so?	vom hochheiligen Paradies. Ist ihm nicht auch?

(Octavian bends over the rose which she holds out to him, then raises his head and looks at her lips.)

SOPHIE

'Tis like a kiss from Heaven. Oh, so sweet and rare that no-one dare breathe it again.	Ist wie ein Gruss vom Himmel. Ist bereits zu stark, als dass man's ertragen kann.
Drawing me on, like something that's tugging at my heart.	Zieht einen nach, als lägen Stricke um das Herz.

(softly)

Where have I been before [29] And felt such rapture?	Wo war ich schon einmal und war so selig?

OCTAVIAN
(at the same time, as though unconscious, and still more softly)

Where have I been before And felt such rapture?	Wo war ich schon einmal und war so selig?

SOPHIE
(with deep expression)

To walk those blessed fields of Paradise once more. I fear not Death itself.	Dahin muss ich zurück! und müsst' ich völlig sterben auf dem Weg!
And yet why dream of death?	Allein ich sterb' ja nicht.
'Tis far, 'tis far, 'tis an eternity That shines on moments of blessedness, Never to be forgotten till death close my eyes.	Das ist ja weit. Ist Zeit und Ewigkeit in einem sel'gen Augenblick, den will ich nie vergessen bis an meinen Tod'.

OCTAVIAN
(at the same time)

I was a child,	Ich war ein Bub
I never heard her voice until today.	da hab' ich die noch nicht gekannt.
But who am I?	Wer bin denn ich?
What fate brings me to her?	Wie komm' denn ich zu ihr?
What fate brings her to me?	Wie kommt denn sie zu mir?
Feeling and sense would leave me, were I not a man;	Wär' ich kein Mann, die Sinne möchten mir vergeh'n.
This is a moment of blessedness,	Das ist ein seliger Augenblick,
Never to be forgotten till death close my eyes.	den will ich nie vergessen bis an meinen Tod'.

(In the meantime Octavian's servants have taken up their position on the left at the back, Faninal's servants with the Major-Domo to the right. Octavian's Footman hands the jewel case to Marianne. Sophie wakes from her reverie and gives the rose to Marianne, who places it in the jewel case. The Footman with the hat approaches Octavian and gives it to him. Octavian's servants withdraw, and at the same time Faninal's servants carry three chairs to the centre, two for Sophie and Octavian, and one for Marianne, further back and to one side. Faninal's Major-Domo carries the jewel case with the rose through the door to the right, the other servants immediately withdraw through the centre doors. Sophie and Octavian stand facing each other, partly restored to the everyday world, but a little embarrassed. At a signal from Sophie both seat themselves, and the Duenna does likewise, at the same moment as the door on the right is locked from the outside by the Major-Domo.)

<table>
<tr><td colspan="2" align="center">SOPHIE</td></tr>
<tr><td>I know you very well, mon cousin!</td><td>[30] Ich kenn' ihn schon recht wohl, mon cousin!</td></tr>
<tr><td colspan="2" align="center">OCTAVIAN</td></tr>
<tr><td>You know me, ma cousine?</td><td>Sie kennt mich, ma cousine?</td></tr>
<tr><td colspan="2" align="center">SOPHIE</td></tr>
<tr><td>Yes, and I've read in the court almanac too,
"The Mirror of Nobility".
I take it every evening up to bed
And read about the Princes and Dukes,
And the Counts who will soon be my relations.</td><td>Ja, aus dem Buch wo die Stammbäumer drin sind,
dem Ehrenspiegel Oesterreichs.
Das nehm' ich immer abends mit in's Bett
und such' mir meine [zu] künft'ge [gräflich' und fürstlich'] Verwandtschaft drin zusammen.</td></tr>
<tr><td colspan="2" align="center">OCTAVIAN</td></tr>
<tr><td>Do you so, ma cousine?</td><td>Tut Sie das, ma cousine?</td></tr>
<tr><td colspan="2" align="center">SOPHIE</td></tr>
<tr><td>I know how old Your Lordship is:
Seventeen and a quarter.
I know all your Christian names: Octavian, Maria Ehrenreich,
Bonaventura, Fernand, Hyacinth.</td><td>Ich weiss, wie alt Euer Liebden sind:
Siebzehn Jahr' und zwei Monat'.
Ich weiss all' Ihre Taufnamen: Octavian, Maria Ehrenreich,
Bonaventura, Fernand, Hyacinth.</td></tr>
<tr><td colspan="2" align="center">OCTAVIAN</td></tr>
<tr><td>I do not know them even half as well.</td><td>So gut weiss ich sie selber nicht einmal.</td></tr>
<tr><td colspan="2" align="center">SOPHIE</td></tr>
<tr><td>I know also...</td><td>Ich weiss noch was.</td></tr>
<tr><td colspan="2" align="center">(blushes)</td></tr>
<tr><td colspan="2" align="center">OCTAVIAN</td></tr>
<tr><td>What do you know, tell me pray, ma cousine?</td><td>Was weiss Sie noch, sag' Sie mir's, ma cousine?</td></tr>
<tr><td colspan="2" align="center">SOPHIE</td></tr>
<tr><td colspan="2" align="center">(not looking at him)</td></tr>
<tr><td>Quinquin.</td><td>Quinquin.</td></tr>
<tr><td colspan="2" align="center">OCTAVIAN</td></tr>
<tr><td colspan="2" align="center">(laughing)</td></tr>
<tr><td>So you know that name too?</td><td>Weiss Sie den Namen auch?</td></tr>
<tr><td colspan="2" align="center">SOPHIE</td></tr>
<tr><td>Men call you Quinquin when they have your friendship,
And lovely ladies, I suppose,
With whom you are acquainted.</td><td>So nennen Ihn halt seine guten Freund'
und schöne Damen, denk'ich mir,
mit denen Er recht gut ist.</td></tr>
<tr><td colspan="2" align="center">(slight pause; naïvely)</td></tr>
<tr><td>I'm happy I'll marry soon! Will you not like it too?
But perhaps you have not given thought to it, mon cousin?
You think, it is another matter happy and free.</td><td>Ich freu' mich auf's Heiraten! Freut Er sich auch darauf?
Oder hat Er leicht noch gar nicht dran gedacht, mon cousin?
Denk' Er: Ist doch was andres als der ledige Stand.</td></tr>
<tr><td colspan="2" align="center">OCTAVIAN</td></tr>
<tr><td colspan="2" align="center">(softly, as she speaks)</td></tr>
<tr><td>What charm she has!</td><td>Wie schön sie ist!</td></tr>
<tr><td colspan="2" align="center">SOPHIE</td></tr>
<tr><td>But then you are a man, and men are what they are.</td><td>Freilich, Er ist ein Mann, da ist Er, was Er bleibt.</td></tr>
</table>

80

| I'll need a husband all my days, to guide my steps; | Ich aber brauch' erst einen Mann, dass ich was bin, |
| And I'll show him my thanks by doing what he tells me. | Dafür bin dich dem Mann dann auch gar sehr verschuldet. |

OCTAVIAN
(deeply moved and softly)

| Oh God, how good and fair she is. | Mein Gott, wie schön und gut sie ist. |
| She quite confuses me. | Sie macht mich ganz verwirrt. |

SOPHIE

I never shall disgrace him, never	Und werd' ihm keine Schand' nicht machen
Forget my rank and station.	und meinen Rang und Vortritt.
Should another wife look down her nose at me	Täte eine, die sich besser dünkt als ich
Or go before me	ihn mir bestreiten
At a Christening or a funeral,	bei einer Kindstauf oder Leich',
I'll show her very quickly,	so will ich, wenn es sein muss,
If needs must be, with a slapped cheek,	mit Ohrfeigen ihr beweisen,
That I am finer bred than she,	das ich die Vornehmere bin
And I'll bear anything rather	und lieber alles hinnehme
Than vulgar pride or insolence!	wie Kränkung oder Ungebühr.

OCTAVIAN
(eagerly)

Ah, do but name the wretch	Wie kann Sie denn nur denken,
Who would presume to hazard such impertinence.	dass man Ihr mit Ungebühr begegnen wird,
For always you'll be the loveliest of all the loveliest creatures.	da Sie [doch] immer die Schönste, die Allerschönste sein wird?

SOPHIE

| You're making fun, mon cousin. | Lacht Er mich aus, mon cousin? |

OCTAVIAN

| What? And why should I laugh? | Wie, glaubt Sie das von mir? |

SOPHIE

You may make fun of me, if you will.	Er darf mich auslachen, wenn Er will.
From you I will gladly take all that you choose,	Von Ihm lass' ich alles mir gerne geschehen,
For I tell you, no gentleman of all I've met with,	weil mir nie noch ein junger Kavalier ...
No, nor dreamed of, has so stolen my heart away as you.	von Nähen oder Weiten also wohlgefallen hat wie Er.
Ah, now he comes. 'Tis my bridegroom to be.	Jetzt aber kommt mein Herr Zukünftiger.

The door at the back is thrown open. All three rise and step to the right. Faninal ceremoniously conducts the Baron over the threshold towards Sophie, giving him precedence. Lerchenau's servants follow in his footsteps, first the Almoner, then the Body Servant. Next comes the Huntsman, with another clownish bumpkin, who has a plaster over his battered nose, and two others, no less uncouth, looking as if they had stepped straight from the turnip-fields into their liveries. All, like their master, carry sprigs of myrtle. Faninal's servants remain in the background. [25]

FANINAL

| May I present now to Your Lordship your bride to be? | Ich präsentiere Euer Gnaden dero Zukünftige. |

BARON
(bowing, then to Faninal)

| Delicious! My compliments to you. | Deliziös! Mach' Ihm mein Kompliment. |

(He kisses Sophie's hand, as if examining it.)

| A wrist so delicate, that is just what I like. | Ein feines Handgelenk. Darauf halt' ich gar viel. |
| Among the middle-classes it is seldom to be found. | Ist unter Bürgerlichen eine selt'ne Distinktion. |

OCTAVIAN
(in an undertone)

| My blood runs hot and cold. | Es wird mir heiss und kalt. |

81

FANINAL

Permit me to present my loyal servant Marianne Leitmetzerin...

(presenting Marianne, who curtsies deeply three times)

Gestatten, dass ich die getreue Jungfer Marianne Leitmetzerin...

BARON

(with a gesture of vexation)

Some other time.
Now come with me while I speak to my Rosenkavalier.

Lass' Er das weg.
Begrüss Er jetzt mit mir meinen Herrn Rosenkavalier.

(He goes with Faninal towards Octavian, and bows. Octavian returns the bow. Lerchenau's servants nearly knock Sophie down, come to a standstill, and retire a couple of paces backwards to the right.)

SOPHIE

(standing on the right with Marianne, in an undertone)

How vulgar his behaviour, he is like a horse-dealer
Who thinks he's bought me at a country fair.

Was sind das für Manieren? Ist er leicht ein Rosstauscher
und kommt ihm vor, er hätt' mich eingekauft?

MARIANNE

(aside)

A cavalier is always unaffected and
Easy in his behaviour,
Tell yourself who he is,
And the rank you will gain,
And soon you will forget your silly ways.

Ein Kavalier hat halt ein ungezwungenes,
leutseliges Betragen.
Sag' dir vor, wer er ist,
und zu was er dich macht,
so werden dir die Faxen gleich vergeh'n.

BARON

(during the foregoing, to Faninal)

It's quite astounding how the young Count resembles someone whom I know.
He has a sister, she's a sweet little bastard.

That is no secret round the Imperial court.

Her Highness told me so herself.

Ist gar zum Staunend, wie der junge Herr jemand gewissem ähnlich sieht:
Hat ein Bastardl, recht ein saub'res, zur Schwester.
Ist kein Geheimnis unter Personen von Stand.
Hab's aus der Fürstin eig' nem Mund,

(genially)

And since our Faninal, now that he's ennobled,
Is one of us in a way
Do not be ashamed, my dear Rofrano,

That your father once sowed his wild oats;
He's not alone in that, he stands with the elite, just like the old Marchese.
I won't deny I've sown some too.

und weil da der Faninal [ja] sozusagen jetzo
zu der Verwandtschaft gehört!
Mach' dir [doch] kein Depit, [darum] Rofrano,
dass dein Vater ein Streichmacher war?
Befindet sich dabei in guter Compagnie, der selige [Herr] Marchese.
Ich selber excludier' mich nicht.

(to Faninal)

Look well now at that long-legged rascal there,
The fair one, at the back.
I cannot point my finger at him,
But you will see at a glance
How he's distinguished by his high-born features.
Is he not truly a splendid fellow?
He has a noble pedigree
But he's the greatest fool of all my household.

Seh' Liebden, schau dir dort den Langen an,
den blonden, hinten dort.
Ich will ihn nicht mit Fingern weisen
aber er sticht wohl hervor
durch eine adelige Contenance.

Ist auch er ein ganz besond'rer Kerl.
Sag's nicht, weil ich der Vater bin,
hat's aber faustdick hinter den Ohren.

SOPHIE

(during the above)

What breeding's this to leave me standing here?
And he is my husband that's to be.
And pock-marked also is his face, on my soul!

Jetzt lässt er mich so steh'n, der grobe Ding!
Und das ist mein Zukünftiger.
Und blattersteppig ist er auch, o mein Gott!

82

MARIANNE

Well, if his front displeases you so, young Mistress Haughty,	Na, wenn er dir von vorn nicht g'fallt, du Jungfer Hochmut,
Then from the back regard him well,	so schau' ihn dir von rückwärts an,
And then you'll find something that is good to see.	da wirst was seh'n, was dir schon g'fallen wird.

SOPHIE

Then tell me what it is that I shall find.	Möcht' wissen, was ich da schon sehen werd'.

MARIANNE
(*mimicking her*)

Then tell me what it is that I shall find.	Möcht' wissen, was sie da schon sehen wird.
Why, that your patron saints have sent you this day	Dass es ein kaiserlicher Kammerer ist,
One of Her Majesty's	den dir dein Schutzpatron
High Chamberlains as bridegroom.	als Herrn Gemahl spendiert hat.
That is very clear to see.	Das kannst seh'n mit einem Blick.

(*The Major-Domo approaches Lerchenau's servants most politely and conducts them out of the room. At the same time Faninal's servants withdraw, except for two, who offer round wine and comfits.*)

FANINAL
(*to the Baron*)

You'll please refresh yourself, it's a very old brandy.	Belieben jetzt vielleicht?–ist ein alter Tokaier.

(*Octavian and the Baron serve themselves.*)

BARON

Good, Faninal, you know what's right and fit,	Brav, Faninal, Er weiss was sich gehört.
To serve such a fine old brandy to toast a fine young daughter.	Serviert einen alten Tokaier zu einem jungen Mädel.
You've done this not too badly.	Ich bin mit ihm zufrieden.

(*to Octavian*)

With two-a-penny nobles like this one, we must show them	Musst denen Bagatelladeligen immer zeigen,
That they are not our equals, you understand me.	dass nicht für unsersgleichen sich ansehen dürfen,
Persons like us have a duty to condescend.	muss immer was von Herablassung dabei sein.

OCTAVIAN
(*pointedly*)

I'm all admiration for Your Lordship!	Ich muss Deine Liebden sehr bewundern.
Your Lordship's manners are so subtle.	Hast wahrhaft grosse Weltmanieren.
You should be sent as an ambassador all over Europe.	Könnt'st einen Embassadeur vorstellen heut' oder morgen.

BARON
(*roughly*)

Come, let me fetch the hussy in.	Ich hol' mir jetzt das Mädl her.
See if she's learned how to talk in company.	Soll uns jetzt Konversation vormachen,
I'll soon discover if she's well informed.	damit ich seh', wie sie beschlagen ist.

(*He takes Sophie by the hand, and leads her back with him.*)

BARON

Eh bien! Now, let us hear you talk, me and your cousin Tavvy.	Eh bien! nun plauder' Sie uns eins, mir und dem Vetter Taverl.
And to begin with, what do you fancy will please you most as a bride?	Sag' Sie heraus, auf was Sie sich halt in der Eh' am meisten freut.

(*The Baron seats himself and tries to make her sit on his lap.*)

SOPHIE
(*pulling away from him*)

What do you mean?	Wo denkt Er hin?

BARON
(at his ease)

Pah! What's my meaning? Let me whisper in your ear.	Pah! Wo ich hindenk'? Komm' Sie da ganz nah zu mir,
And I will tell you frankly all my meaning.	dann will ich Ihr erzählen, wo ich hindenk'.

(Same business. Sophie pulls more angrily away from him.)

BARON
(at his ease)

Would my lady prefer it if I were to play	Wär Ihr leicht präferabel, dass man gegen Ihrer
The dancing-master, bowing and cavorting?	den Ceremonienmeister sollt' hervortun?
With "mille pardons" and "devotion",	Mit "mille pardons" und "devotion",
And "By your leave", and "My respects"?	und "Geh da weg" und "hab Respeck"?

SOPHIE

Undoubtedly, yes, 'twould surely be much better!	Wahrhaftig und ja gefiele mir das besser!

BARON
(laughing)

Not for me! I tell you! None of that for me, miss!	Mir auch nicht! Das sieht Sie! Mir auch ganz und gar nicht!
I am an open-hearted country lad, I like a free and easy life.	Bin einer biedern offenherzigen Galanterie recht zugetan.

(He starts to kiss her, but she energetically pushes him away.)

FANINAL
(offering Octavian the second chair, which he refuses)

How can it be? There sits a Lerchenau	Wie ist mir denn! Da sitzt ein Lerchenau
And sets his heart upon our little Sophie, the rascals might be man and wife.	und karessiert in Ehrbarkeit mein Sopherl, als wär' sie ihm schon angetraut.
And there stands a Rofrano, makes as if at home–	Und da steht ein Rofrano, grad' als müsst's so sein–
A Count Rofrano, nothing less,	Ein Graf Rofrano, sonsten nix–
And brother to Her Majesty's Lord High Rod.	der Bruder vom Marchese Obersttruchsess.

OCTAVIAN
(angrily, aside)

There's a rude fellow. There's nothing I'd like better	Das ist ein Kerl, dem möcht ich wo begegnen
Than once to catch him	mit meinem Degen da,
Sword in hand and no-one by to watch.	wo ihn kein Wachter schreien hört'.
No, nothing better in the world.	Ja, das ist alles was ich möcht'.

SOPHIE
(to the Baron)

Let go of me. We are not married yet!	Ei lass Er doch, wir sind nicht so vertraut!

BARON
(to Sophie)

My dear, are you shy before Cousin Tavvy?	Geniert Sie sich leicht vor dem Vetter Taverl?
Don't be so foolish.	Da hat Sie Unrecht.
Why, you know in Paris,	Hör' Sie, in Paris
Where they have the very finest manners,	wo doch die hohe Schul' ist für Manieren,
There is naught	[da] gibt's frei nichts,
That may be done by newly married folk,	was unter jungen Eheleuten geschieht,
To which 'tis not usual to invite your friends to watch you,	wozu man nicht Einladungen liess ergeh'n zum Zuschau'n,
Even the King himself does.	ja an den König selber.

FANINAL
(aside)

Would that my palace were of glass,	Wär' nur die Mauer da von Glas,
Every pettifogging burgess in the town,	dass alle bürgerlichen Neidhammeln von Wien
Jaundiced with envy should see them sit *en famille.*	sie en famille beisammen so sitzen seh'n!

| For that pleasure I'd give my richest house right gladly, 'pon my soul. | Dafür wollt' ich mein Lerchenfelder Eckhaus geben, meiner Seel'! |

OCTAVIAN
(furious)

| How can I bear to watch him there, So coarse, so unashamed with her. [*lit.* I would repent of all my sins.] Would I could fly away from here! | Dass ich das Mannsbild sehen muss, so frech, so unverschämt mit ihr. [Ich büss' all' meine Sünden ab!] Könnt' ich hinaus und fort von hier! |

(The Baron grows more and more importunate; Sophie is at her wits' end.)

BARON
(to Sophie)

| Don't be so silly now, for you belong to me! It's all right. Now be good! It's all just as I planned it! | Lass' Sie die Flausen nur! Gehört doch jetzo mir! Geht's all recht! Sei Sie gut! Geht all's so wie am Schnürl! |

(half to himself, fondling her)

Suits me exactly! Tender as a chicken!	Ganz meine Massen! Schultern wie ein Henderl!
Quite skinny though–no matter, and so white,	Hundsmager noch–das macht nichts, aber weiss
White as driven snow. There's nothing I like more!	mit einem Glanz [darauf] wie ich ihn ästimier!
I have the luck of all the Lerchenaus!	Ich hab' halt ja ein lerchenauisch Glück!

(Sophie tears herself away and stamps her foot.)

BARON
(delighted)

| Gad! She's a fine little peppery spitfire! | Ist Sie ein rechter Capricenschädel! |

(rises and runs after her)

| And see how hot her cheeks are burning, Hot enough to burn your hands! | Steigt Ihr das Blut gar in die Wangen, dass man sich die Hand verbrennt? |

SOPHIE
(flushing with anger)

| Take off your hands from me! | Lass' Er die Hand davon! |

(Octavian in silent anger, crushes the glass he holds in his hand, and throws the pieces to the ground.)

MARIANNE

(She runs with affected grace towards Octavian, picks up the pieces, and confides her delight to him.)

| He has uncommon easy ways, the Herr Baron! He's quite enchanting, such originality! | Ist recht ein familiärer Mann, der Herr Baron! Man delektiert sich, was er all's für Einfäll' hat! |

BARON
(near Sophie)

| Nothing suits me better. No kind of simperings or tender airs Could give me half such pleasure on my soul! | Geht mir nichts darüber! Könnt' mich mit Schmachterei und Zärtlichkeit nicht halb so glüchlick machen, meiner Seel'! |

SOPHIE
(furious, to his face)

| I hardly care if I please you or not! | Ich denk' nicht dran, dass ich ihn glücklich mach'! |

BARON
(complacently)

| You please me fine, no matter if you like it or you don't. | Sie wird es tun, ob Sie daran wird denken oder nicht. |

OCTAVIAN
(aside, pale with anger)

| Ah! I must go without farewell! Or else I cannot tell Just what I might be led to do! Oh! I can stay no longer! I must go! | Hinaus! Hinaus! Und kein Adieu! Sonst steh' ich nicht dafür, dass ich nicht was Verwirrtes tu! Hinaus aus diesen Stuben! Nur hinaus! |

(In the meantime the Notary has entered with his Clerk, introduced by Faninal's Major-Domo. He announces them in a whisper to Faninal. Faninal goes towards the Notary at the back, speaks to him, and looks through a bundle of documents which the Clerk presents to him.)

SOPHIE
(between her teeth)

There is no man has ever dared to speak to me like this.	Hat nie kein Mann dergleichen Reden nicht zu mir geführt!
What can you think of me, and of yourself?	Möcht' wissen was ihn dünkt von mir und ihm?
What are you, Sir, to me?	Was ist Er denn zu mir?

BARON
(contentedly)

You'll find out overnight	Wird kommen über Nacht,
That you have learned	dass Sie ganz sanft,
With pleasure what I am to you.	wird wissen, was ich bin zu Ihr.
Just like the little song–you surely know it?	Ganz wie's im Liedel heisst–kennt Sie das Liedel?
Lalalalala– [31]	Lalalalala–

(very sentimentally)

My love shall be yours all in all!	wie ich dein Alles werde sein!
With me, with me you will find no room too small,	Mit mir, mit mir keine Kammer dir zu klein,
Without me, without me, every day is so long,	ohne mich, ohne mich jeder Tag dir so bang,

(impudently and coarsely)

With me, with me never night long enough. [32]	mit mir, mit mir keine Nacht dir zu lang!

(As he tries to draw Sophie still closer to him, she frees herself, and violently pushes him back.)

MARIANNE
(hurrying to Sophie)

He has uncommon easy ways, the Herr Baron!	Ist recht ein familiärer Mann, der Herr Baron!
He's quite enchanting, such originality!	Man delektiert sich, was er all's für Einfäll' hat!

(nervously and excitedly)

Such originality, the Herr Baron!	Nein was er all's für Einfäll' hat, der Herr Baron!

OCTAVIAN
(without looking, and yet aware of all that is going on)

It's more than I can stomach!	Ich steh' auf glüh'nden Kohlen!
I stand on coals of fire!	Ich fahr' aus meiner Haut!
I'm doing penance in an hour	Ich büss' in dieser einen Stund'
For many years of sin!	all' meine Sünden ab!

BARON
(aside, very contended)

I always did say, I have all the luck [33] of the Lerchenaus.	Wahrhaftig und ja, ich hab' halt ein lerchenauisch Glück!
There is naught in the world tickles my appetite	Gibt gar nichts auf der Welt, was mich so enflammiert
And gives me back again my youth like a defiant wench.	und also vehement verjüngt als wie ein rechter Trotz!

(Faninal and the Notary, followed by the Clerk, have advanced to the front left of the stage. As soon as he sees the Notary, the Baron addresses Sophie eagerly, without the slightest idea what she is thinking.)

But now there's work to do: You must do without me.	Dort gibt's Geschäfte jetzt, muss mich dispensieren:
They need my help in there.	bin dort von Wichtigkeit. Indessen
And meanwhile there's cousin Tavvy who will entertain you!	der Vetter Taverl leistet Ihr Gesellschaft!

FANINAL

Is it now convenient, dear son-in-law?	Wenn's jetzt belieben tät, Herr Schwiegersohn!

86

BARON
(*eagerly*)

Of course it's convenient.	Natürlich wird's belieben.

(*In passing, to Octavian, touching him familiarly*)

I've no objection,	Hab's nicht dawider,
If you would like to flirt a little, Cousin,	wenn du ihr möchtest Äugerl machen, Vetter,
Now or at any time.	jetzt oder künftighin.
She's still a little touch-me-not.	Ist noch ein rechter Rühr-nicht-an.
The more she learns from you, the better it will please me.	Betracht's als förderlich, je mehr sie degourdiert wird.
You can see that the girl is like an unbroken foal.	Ist wie bei einem jungen ungerittenen Pferd.
The husband has the better bargain in the end,	Kommt all's dem Angetrauten letzterdings zu Gut',
So long as he's wise enough to exercise his matrimonial rights.	wofern er sein eh'lich Privilegium zu Nutz zu machen weiss.

(*The Baron goes to the left. The servant who had admitted the Notary has in the meantime opened the door on the left. Faninal and the Notary make for the door. The Baron fixes his eyes on Faninal, and indicates to him that he must keep a distance of three paces. Faninal obsequiously retreats. The Baron takes precedence, assures himself that Faninal is three paces behind him, and walks solemnly through the door on the left. Faninal follows, and after him come the Notary and his Clerk. The Footman closes the door on the left, and goes out, leaving the door leading to the ante-room open. The Footman who was serving refreshments has retired. Sophie stands on the right, confused and humiliated. Marianne curtseys in the direction of the door until it closes. Octavian, quivering with excitement, hurries over to Sophie, glancing back to make sure the others have gone.*)*

OCTAVIAN

And will you really wed that bumpkin, ma cousine?	Wird Sie das Mannsbild da heiraten, ma cousine?

SOPHIE
(*taking a step towards him, in a whisper*)

Not for the world!	Nichtum die Welt!

(*glancing at her Duenna*)

Oh, God! Could we but be alone,	Mein Gott, wär' ich allein mit Ihm,
That I might beg of you, that I might beg of you!	dass ich Ihn bitten könnt'! dass ich Ihn bitten könnt'!

OCTAVIAN
(*quickly, in an undertone*)

What is it you would beg of me? Tell me now, quick!	Was ist's, dass Sie mich bitten möcht'? Sag' Sie mir's schnell!

SOPHIE
(*taking another step towards him*)

Oh my God, I implore your aid! And you will not help me because	O mein Gott, dass Er mir halt hilft! Und Er wird mir nicht helfen wollen
He is your cousin and your friend.	Weil Er halt sein Vetter ist!

OCTAVIAN
(*vehemently*)

He is cousin by courtesy;	Nenn' ihn Vetter aus Höflichkeit;
Praised be God above,	Gott sei Lob und Dank,
I never saw him in my life until this time yesterday.	hab' ihn im Leben vor dem gestrigen Tage nie geseh'n!

(*Some of the servant girls rush headlong across the anteroom hotly pursued by Lerchenau's attendants. The Body Servant and the servant with the plaster on his nose are at the heels of a pretty young girl, and corner her close by the salon door.*)

FANINAL'S MAJOR-DOMO
(*running in much perturbed, calling the Duenna to help him*)

His Lordship's servants, drunk as a lord, by your leave, Ma'am,	Die Lerchenauischen sind voller Branntwein gesoffen
Are scaring our girls to death, twenty times worse than	und geh'n aufs Gesindel los, zwanzigmal ärger
The Turks, Ma'am, or Croatians.	als Türken und Crowaten!

MARIANNE

Fetch up our people to help you, where can they be?	Hol' Er [von] unsere[n] Leut[en], wo sind denn die?

(She runs off with the Major-Domo. They rescue the girl from her assailants and lead her away. All disappear. The anteroom remains empty.)

SOPHIE
(speaking freely now that she is unobserved)

My trust is in your kindness, mon cousin,	[34] Zu Ihm hätt' ich ein Zutrau'n, mon cousin,
Kindness like no-one's in the world.	so wie zu niemand auf der Welt,
Ah, you could be my saviour,	dass Er mir könnte helfen
If you only had the will to be!	wenn Er nur den guten Willen hätt'!

OCTAVIAN

First you must yourself take courage,	Erst muss Sie sich selber helfen,
Then I too will help:	dann hilf ich Ihr auch.
Till you do that yourself	Tu' Sie das erst für sich,
I can do naught for you.	Dann tu' ich was für Sie!

SOPHIE
(confidingly, almost tenderly)

What do you mean, what is it I must do?	Was ist denn das, was ich zuerst muss tun?

OCTAVIAN
(softly)

You know that already!	Das wird Sie wohl wissen!

SOPHIE
(looking at him undismayed)

And what is it that you will do for me?	Und was ist das, was Er für mich will tun,
Ah, tell me pray!	O sag' Er mir's!

OCTAVIAN
(with determination)

Now you must stand alone and fight for us both!	Nun muss Sie ganz allein für uns zwei einsteh'n!

SOPHIE

What? For us both?	Wie? für uns zwei?
O say that again!	O sag' Er's noch einmal.

OCTAVIAN
(softly)

For us both!	Für uns zwei!

SOPHIE
(rapturously)

In all my life I have never heard that word!	Ich hab' im Leben so was Schönes nicht gehört!

OCTAVIAN
(louder)

For you and me you must be steadfast and still be–	Für sich und mich muss Sie sich wehren und bleiben–

SOPHIE

Still be?	Bleiben?

OCTAVIAN

What you are.	Was Sie ist.

(Sophie takes his hand, bends over it, and kisses it quickly before he can withdraw it. He kisses her on the lips and holds her as she nestles up to him; tenderly)

With eyes all veiled by your tears	[35] Mit Ihren Augen voll[er] Tränen
You're asking my aid, your fears have pierced my heart,	Kommt Sie zu mir, damit Sie sich beklagt,
Be brave! Nothing shall touch or hurt you,	vor Angst muss Sie an mich sich lehnen,
Your tender heart is full of fear.	Ihr armes Herz ist ganz verzagt.
Now I must find a way to make you trust me,	Und ich muss jetzt als Ihren Freund mich zeigen
And yet I know now how!	und weiss noch gar nicht, wie!
Rapture so blessed, so wondrous	Mir ist so selig, so eigen
To hold you here in my arms.	dass ich Dich halten darf:
Give answer, but only with silence:	Gieb Antwort, aber gieb sie mit Schweigen:
Did you come of your own free will to find me?	Bist Du von selber so zu mir gekommen?

88

Say yes or no. Say yes or no.	Ja oder nein? Ja oder nein?
You cannot find the words to tell it.	Du musst es nicht mit Worten sagen–
Say, was it done from choice?	Hast Du es gern getan?
Say, was it just your need?	Sag', oder nur aus Not?
Just your need that bade you offer me such marvels,	Nur aus Not so alles zu mir hergetragen,
Your heart, your lovely, lovely face?	Dein Herz, Dein liebliches Gesicht?
Say, can it be that long ago	Sag', ist Dir nicht, dass irgendwo
In some divine remembered dream,	in irgend einem schönen Traum
We lived this hour before?	das einmal schon so war?
Think you not so?	Spürst Du's wie ich?
Say, think you not as I?	Sag': spürst Du's so wie ich?
My heart and soul by your side are staying,	Mein Herz und Seel' wird bei Ihr bleiben,
Wheresoe'er you are,	wo Sie geht und steht,
For all eternity.	bis in alle Ewigkeit.

SOPHIE

What rapture! Your strong arms enfold me	Ich möchte mich bei Ihm verstecken
And hide me ever from the world.	und nichts mehr wissen von der Welt.
When I can feel your heart so close to mine,	Wenn Er mich so in Seinen Armen hält,
Nothing in life is harsh or dreadful.	kann mich nichts Hässliches erschrecken.
I want to stay there, there!	Da bleiben möcht' ich, da!
In silence, and let what may befall,	Und schweigen, und was mir auch gescheh',
Deep hidden like a linnet in the branches,	geborgen wie der Vogel in den Zweigen,
Breathless beside you!	stillsteh'n und spüren:
You, you are close at hand!	Er, Er ist in der Näh'!
My heart should fail me now for fear and grief,	Mir müsste angst und bang im Herzen sein,
But no, I feel only joy and blessedness	statt dessen fühl' ich nur Freud und Seligkeit
And nothing more,	und keine Pein,
I cannot find the words to tell it!	ich könnt' es nicht mit Worten sagen!
Have I been sinful in what I did?	Hab'ich was Unrechtes getan?
I sought you in my need!	Ich war halt in der Not!
Your arms were so near!	Da war Er mir nah!
I looked upon your face,	Da war es Sein Gesicht,
Your eyes, your manly grace	Sein Auge jung und licht,
And then I knew my place	auf das ich mich gericht
Was at hand by your side;	Sein liebes Gesicht–
Since that moment I know not	Und seitdem weiss ich halt nichts–
What I feel any more.	Nichts mehr von mir.
Stay, stay close to me,	Bleib' Er nur bei mir
Protect me, save me, stay beside me,	Er muss mir Seinen Schutz vergönnen,
I follow where'er you guide me,	was Er will, werd'ich können:
Save me, leave me not.	bleib nur Er bei mir!
Protect me now and stay beside me,	Er muss mir Seinen Schutz vergönnen,
With your protective arms around me–	was Er wird wollen, werd'ich können–
Stay near me, stay ever close by my side.	bleib' Er nur bei mir.

From the secret doors in the rear corners Valzacchi and Annina emerge noiselessly, and watch the lovers. They approach silently on tiptoe. Octavian draws Sophie to him to kiss her; by this time the Italians are right behind them. They duck behind the armchairs. Then they rush out from their hiding-places. Annina seizes Sophie, Valzacchi takes hold of Octavian.

VALZACCHI AND ANNINA
(*screaming*)

Herr Baron von Lerchenau!–Herr Baron von Lerchenau!	Herr Baron von Lerchenau!–Herr Baron von Lerchenau!

(*Octavian starts aside to the right.*)

VALZACCHI
(*holding him with difficulty, breathlessly to Annina*)

Run, and fetch de Barone!	Lauf und 'ole Seine Gnade!
Now at once! I must 'old on tight to him!	Snell, nur snell. Ik muss 'alten diese 'err!

If I let go of her, she will be off! | Lass' ich die Fräulein aus, läuft sie mir weg!

BOTH

Herr Baron von Lerchenau, | Herr Baron von Lerchenau,
Herr Baron von Lerchenau! | Herr Baron von Lerchenau!
Come and see your bride to be | Komm' zu seh'n die Fräulein Braut!
Beside her Rosenkavalier! | Mit eine junge Cavalier!
Come here quickly, come here quickly! | Kommen eilig, kommen hier! Ecco!
Ecco!

(The Baron enters from the door on the left, the Italians let their victims go, spring aside, bow low to the Baron with significant gestures. The Baron with folded arms contemplates the group. Ominous pause. Sophie nestles timidly up to Octavian.)

BARON

Eh bien, Mamsell, what have you got to tell me? | Eh bien, Mamsell, was hat Sie mir zu sagen?

(Sophie says nothing. The Baron shows no signs of losing his composure.)

Well, do not hesitate! | Nun, resolvier' Sie sich!

SOPHIE

Oh God, what can I tell you? | Mein Gott, was soll sie sagen:
You would not understand! | Er wird mich nicht versteh'n!

BARON
(genially)

I'll be the judge of that. | Das werden wir ja seh'n!

OCTAVIAN
(moving a step nearer to the Baron)

'Tis my duty to inform Your Lordship | Eu'r Liebden muss ich halt vermelden,
A most essential change has taken place | dass sich in seiner Angelgenheit
Concerning Fräulein Faninal. | was wichtiges verändert hat!

BARON
(genially)

Oh really? Change? None that I know! | Verändert? Ei, nicht dass ich wüsst'!

OCTAVIAN

And therefore I now have to tell you! | Darum soll Er es jetzt erfahren!
The Lady— | Die Fräulein—

BARON

He! You're not so slow! You've learned your lessson early | Ei, Er ist nicht faul! Er weiss zu profitieren,
In spite of being so young, I must congratulate you! | mit Seinen siebzehn Jahr'! Ich muss Ihm gratulieren!

OCTAVIAN

The Lady— | Die Fräulein—

BARON
(half to himself)

I was just the same when I was your age, | Ist mir ordentlich, ich seh' mich selber!
You rascal! How you make me laugh, you poodle-puppy! | Muss lachen über den Filou, den pudeljungen.

OCTAVIAN

The Lady— | Die Fräulein—

BARON

She's dumb, I presume, and so she's chosen you | Ei! Sie ist wohl stumm und hat Ihn angestellt
To speak as her attorney! | für Fräulein—

OCTAVIAN

The Lady— | Die Fräulein—
(He breaks off once more, as if to allow Sophie to speak.)

SOPHIE
(terrorstruck)

No! No! I cannot speak the word. | Nein! Nein! Ich bring' den Mund nicht auf.
You speak for me! | Sprech Er für mich!

OCTAVIAN
(with determination)

The Lady— | Die Fräulein—

90

BARON
(*mimicking him*)

The Lady, The Lady! The Lady! The Lady!	Die Fräulein, Die Fräulein! Die Fräulein! Die Fräulein!
It's like a cheap little comedy. It bores me!	ist eine Kreuzerkomödi wahrhaftig!
So now be off with you before I lose my patience.	Jetzt echappier' Er sich, sonst reisst mir die Geduld.

OCTAVIAN
(*very determined*)

The Lady, in a word, The Lady does not like you.	Die Fräulein, kurz und gut die Fräulein mag Ihn nicht.

BARON
(*genially*)

Never mind about that. She will like what I teach her.	Sei Er da ausser Sorg'. Wird schon lernen mich mögen.

(*moving towards Sophie*)

Come with me to the lawyer who will need you soon to sign the marriage papers.	Komm' Sie da jetzt hinein: wird gleich an Ihrer sein die Unterschrift zu geben.

SOPHIE
(*retreating*)

No, not for all the world will I go in with you!	Um keinen Preis geh' ich an Seiner Hand hinein!
How can a cavalier be so indelicate!	Wie kann ein Cavalier so ohne Zartheit sein!

OCTAVIAN
(*now between the other two and the left-hand door, very emphatically*)

'Tis clear enough! The Lady's mind is now made up;	Versteht Er deutsch? Die Fräulein hat sich resolviert
She says she will let Your Lordship stay unmarried	Sie will Euer Gnaden ungeheirat' lassen
For now and evermore.	in Zeit und Ewigkeit!

BARON
(*with the air of a man in a great hurry*)

Nonsense! Baby talk! You're puffing like a cow in labour.	Mancari! Jungfernred' ist nicht gehau'n und nicht gestochen!
It's time to go!	Verlaub' Sie jetzt!

(*He takes Sophie by the hand.*)

OCTAVIAN
(*planting himself firmly in front of the door*)

If one spark you have in you Of true gentility Then what I just have told you Makes your duty quite clear.	Wenn nur so viel in Ihm ist von einem Cavalier so wird Ihm wohl genügen, was Er g'hört hat von mir!

BARON
(*to Sophie, as if he had not heard*)

Thank your lucky stars I choose to close one eye,	Gratulier' Sie sich nur, dass ich ein Aug' zudrück'!
As is correct and seemly for a gentleman!	Daran mag Sie erkennen, was ein Cavalier ist!

(*He attempts to go past Octavian with her.*)

OCTAVIAN
(*grasping his sword*)

There's a way to make my meaning Understood by such as you are!	Wird doch [wohl] ein Mittel geben, seinesgleichen zu bedeuten!

BARON
(*not letting go of Sophie, and pushing her towards the door*)

That I can scarce believe!	Ei, schwerlich, wüsste nicht!

OCTAVIAN
(*losing all self-control*)

Of the name of gentleman You are unworthy, Sir!	Ich acht' Ihn mit nichten für einen Cavalier!

BARON
(pompously)

Indeed, were I not sure you know what is my due,
And were you not a kinsman, I hardly could, I vow,
Restrain myself from measures of violence!

Wahrhaftig wüsst' ich nicht, dass Er mich respectiert,
und wär' Er nicht verwandt, es wär mir jetzo schwer,
das ich mit Ihm nicht übereinander käm!

(He attempts with feigned unconcern to lead Sophie towards the centre doors, after the Italians have signalled to him energetically to go that way.)

Come now, go to your dear beloved father;

Komm' Sie! Geh'n zum Herrn Vater dort hinüber!

You will find him waiting in there!

Ist bereits der nähere Weg!

OCTAVIAN
(following him, close to Sophie)

I trust you don't forget you've a name to defend.
I know a most convenient garden.

Ich hoff', Er kommt vielmehr jetzt mit mir hinters Haus,
ist dort ein recht bequemer Garten.

BARON
(continuing in the same direction, still feigning unconcern, trying to lead Sophie away, and still holding her by the hand. Over his shoulder.)

God bless my soul, it's not convenient now.
The attorney must not be kept waiting.
'Twould be impolite to my little bride.

Bewahre. Wär' mir jetzo nicht genehm.
Lass um All's den Notari nicht warten.
Wär' gar ein Affront für die Jungfer Braut!

OCTAVIAN
(pulling his coat sleeve)

By Satan, never was a hide so thick!
And through the door I'll not let you pass!
I tell you flatly to your face
I think you're a rascally knave
And a fortune-hunter.
You are a scoundrelly liar, a dirty old peasant,
And a cur without honour or shame!
If need be I'll make you learn on the spot the truth!

Beim Satan, Er hat eine dicke Haut!
Auch dort die Tür passiert Er mir nicht!
Ich schrei's Ihm jetzt in Sein Gesicht:
ich acht' Ihn für einen Filou,
einen Mitgift jäger,
einen durchtriebenen Lügner und schmutzigen Bauer,
einen Kerl ohne Anstand und Ehr'!
Und wenn's sein muss, geb' ich Ihm auf dem Fleck die Lehr'!

(Sophie has freed herself from the Baron, and takes refuge behind Octavian. They stand on the left, almost in front of the door.)

BARON
(puts two fingers in his mouth and gives a shrill whistle.)

This little boy of ours at seventeen
Has learned a pretty turn of speech.

Was so ein Bub' in Wien mit siebzehn Jahr
schon für ein vorlaut' Mundwerk hat!

(looking towards the centre door)

But God be praised that everyone in Vienna

Doch Gott sei Lob, man kennt in hiesiger Stadt

Knows just who I am,
And that includes, of course, Her Majesty the Queen!
One is just what one is, and there's no need to prove it.
You'll allow me to bid you good day, Sir, and let me pass.

den Mann, der vor ihm steht,
halt bis hinauf zu kaiserlicher Majestät!
Man ist halt, was man ist und braucht's nicht zu beweisen.
Dass lass'Er sich gesagt sein und geb' mir den Weg [da] frei.

(All Lerchenau's servants have marched in through the centre door. The Baron, glancing to the back once more, assures himself of their presence. He approaches Sophie and Octavian, determined to secure both Sophie and his retreat.)

I would be most upset if all my servants yonder–

Wär' mir wahrhaftig leid wenn meine Leut da hinten–

OCTAVIAN
(furious)

So you have made your mind up to seek help from
Your grooms and lackeys in our affair.
Then draw, Sir, or commend your soul!

Ah, untersteht Er, seine Bedienten
hineinzumischen in unsern Streit!
Jetzt zieh' Er oder Gnad' Ihm Gott!

(He draws his sword. The Baron's servants, who had already approached a few steps, hesitate

when they see what is happening, and pause in their advance. The Baron takes a step to secure Sophie.)

Draw, Satan, draw now, or on my sword
I'll spit you!

Zu Satan, zieh' Er oder ich stech' Ihn
nieder!

SOPHIE
SOPHIE

Ah, God, oh what will happen next?

O Gott, was wird denn jetzt gescheh'n?

BARON
(withdraws a step)

Before a lady, shame! Come now, behave
yourself!

Vor einer Dame, pfui! So sei Er doch
gescheit!

(Octavian rushes at him furiously. The Baron draws, lunges clumsily, and receives the point of Octavian's sword in his arm, above the elbow. All the Baron's servants rush on Octavian. He springs aside to the right and keeps them at arm's length, whirling his sword about him. The Almoner, Valzacchi and Annina hurry to the Baron, and, supporting him, lead him to one of the chairs in the middle of the room.)

BARON
(dropping his sword)

Help! Help! I'm stuck, I'm bleeding!
Murder! Murder! Murder!

Mord! Mord! Mein' Blut! Zu Hilfe!
Mörder! Mörder! Mörder!

(surrounded by his servants and the Italians, who hide him from the audience)

I'm feeling feverish! Go, call a doctor!

Ich hab' ein hitzig Blut! Um Arzt'! um
Leinwand!

Some bandage! And call the police! I ... I'm
bleeding to death! I'm dead!

Verband her! Ich verblut' mich auf eins,
zwei! [drei!]

Don't let him go! And call the police!
And call the police!

Aufhalten den! Um Polizei! Um Polizei!

LERCHENAU'S SERVANTS
(closing around Octavian with more swagger than courage)

Break his crown! Lay hold there!
Spider webs! Get a sponge!
Quick, take his sword away!
Stick him dead, through the heart!

Den haut's z'samm! den haut's z'samm!
Spinnweb' her! Feuerschwamm!
Reisst's ihm den Spadi weg!
Schlagt's ihn tot auf' m Fleck!

(All Faninal's servants, female domestics, kitchen staff, and stable hands, have streamed in through the centre door.)

ANNINA
(haranguing the servants)

Yes, zis young gentleman
And ze lady, understand?
Vere already in secret
Familiar, understand?

Der junge Cavalier
und die Fräulein Braut, versteht's?
Waren im Geheimen
schon recht vertraut, versteht's?

(Valzacchi and the Almoner divest the Baron of his coat. The latter groans uninterruptedly.)

FANINAL'S SERVANTS

Somebody wounded? Who?
The stranger there?
Which one? The son-in-law?
Seize the brawler, hold him tight!
Who is it that first did draw?
That one all dressed in white!
Who, the Count that brought the rose?
For what cause, then? Just for her!
Hold him tight! Tan his hide!
Just for the bride?
They were a-courting!
We'll make him rue it!
Look at the brazen thing!
How dared she do it?

G'stochen is einer? Wer?
Der dort? Der fremde Herr?
Welcher? Der Bräutigam?
Packt's den Duellanten z'samm!
Welcher is der Duellant?
Der dort im weissen G'wand!
Wer? Der Rosenkavalier?
Wegen was denn? Wegen ihr!
Angepackt! Niederg'haut!
Wegen der Braut?
Wegen der Liebschaft!
Wütender Hass is!
Schaut's nur die Fräulein an,
schaut's wie sie blass is!

MARIANNE
(clearing a way for herself to the Baron. All press around him)

Such a high-born Lord! Such a cruel sword!
Such a heavy blow! Such an awful day!

So ein fescher Herr! So ein' gross' Malheur!
So ein schwerer Schlag! So ein Unglückstag!

OCTAVIAN
(holding his assailants at arm's length)

Short shrift for all who

Wer mir zu nah kommt,

93

Come too near me!	der lernt beten!
I will explain all	Was da passiert ist,
When you can hear me!	kann ich vertreten!

SOPHIE
(*front left*)

Oh, what confusion is this!	Alles geht durcheinand!
Wondrous! Quicker than lightning	Furchtbar war's, wie ein Blitz!
He drove them all away!	Wie er's erzwungen hat!
I feel naught but the thrill	Ich spür' nur seine Hand,
Of his embraces still!	die mich umschlungen hat!
I feel nothing of fear,	Ich verspür' nichts von Angst,
I feel nothing of shame;	ich verspür' nichts von Schmerz,
His bright glances have consumed	nur das Feuer, seinen Blick
All my heart with their flame!	durch und durch, bis ins Herz!

LERCHENAU'S SERVANTS
(*desisting from attacking Octavian, they go up to the maids nearest them, whom they proceed to handle roughly*)

Linen bands we're needing!	Leinwand her! Verband machen!
Sponges to staunch the bleeding!	Fetzen aus'n Gewand machen!
Bring us quickly salve and plaster,	Vorwärts, keine Spanponaden!
Bring them quick for our dear Master!	Leinwand her für Seine Gnaden!

SOPHIE
(*calling in despair to Octavian*)

| Dearest! | Liebster! |

OCTAVIAN
(*calling in despair to Sophie*)

| Dearest! | Liebste! |

(*Faninal rushes in through the door to the left, followed by the Notary and his Clerk, who remain standing by the door in great alarm. Lerchenau's Servants make as if to tear the clothes off the younger and prettier maidservants near them. Mêlée, until Faninal begins.*)

BARON
(*who can be heard, but hardly seen*)

I can see other people's blood unmoved, my	Ich kann ein jedes Blut mit Ruhe fliessen
own makes me flinch!	sehen,
My own makes me flinch! Oh! oh!	nur bloss das meinig nicht! oh! oh!

(*shouting at the Duenna*)

Stop shouting and act for once. Stand by	So tu' Sie doch was g'scheidt's, so rett'
for I am dying.	Sie doch mein Leben!
Oh! Oh!	Oh! Oh!

ANNINA
(*in front, to the left, curtseying, crossing eagerly over to Faninal*)

The gentleman and Miss	Der junge Cavalier
Are united, Your Honour,	und die Fräulein Braut, Gnaden,
They have been in secrecy	waren im Geheimen
Plighted, Your Honour!	schon recht vertraut, Gnaden!
Full of devotion	Wir voller Eifer
And care for Your Honour,	für'n Herrn Baron, Gnaden,
We have kept respectfully	haben sie betreten
Watch upon the pair, yes, Sir.	in aller Devotion, Gnaden!

(*Marianne rushes out, and after a brief interlude, returns breathless, laden with linen, followed by two maids with sponges and basins. They surround the Baron and busy themselves about him. Sophie, as soon as she sees her father, runs over to the right, and stands by Octavian's side. The latter sheathes his sword.*)

MARIANNE
(*busy about the Baron*)

| Such a high-born Lord! Such a cruel sword! | So ein fescher Herr! So ein' gross' Malheur! |
| Such a heavy blow! Such an awful day! | So ein schwerer Schlag! So ein Unglückstag! |

FANINAL
(*He is at first speechless. Then he throws his hands over his head and bursts out.*)

Dear son-in-law, what's happening here?	Herr Schwiegersohn! Wie ist Ihm denn?
The Saints preserve us!	Mein Herr und Heiland!
What an ill-bred affray, here in my house of	Dass Ihm in mein' Palais das hat passieren
all things!	müssen!

94

Has no-one fetched the surgeon yet? You rogues, you!
Take my ten horses. Ride them all to death!
How is it none of you mustered the wit
To throw yourselves between them? Do I stuff
A whole troop of liveried imbeciles only for disgrace
To fall on me, and on my brand new palace too?

(going up to Octavian)

This is not the behaviour I had expected
Your Lordship would affect!

BARON
(groaning)

Oh! Oh!

FANINAL
(turning to the Baron)

Oh, that such blood of priceless pedigree
should run to waste like this!

(to Octavian)

O pah! Oh! What a common, vulgar butchery!

BARON

I have blood so young, so full of fire,
Nothing can staunch it! Oh!

FANINAL
(venting his anger on Octavian in restrained irony)

Truly from Your most noble Lordship your incomparable wit
Should make a better show of taste and breeding!

OCTAVIAN
(politely)

I beg you to forgive me.
I am so deeply grieved that this thing should have happened.
But I am not to blame. I promise in the fullness of time,
Your Honour will discharge me without sentence;
You'll hear from your own daughter's lips.

FANINAL
(controlling himself with difficulty)

'Tis well, Sir. Come now, tell me!

SOPHIE
(determined)

As you command me, father. I shall unfold my story.
My Lord there has not acted as a man of honour.

FANINAL
(angrily)

How, of whom do you speak? Of my future son-in-law?
If that is so, I beg you think e'er you speak.

SOPHIE
(quietly)

It is not so. I cannot give my hand to him.

Gelaufen um den Medicus! Geflogen!

Meine zehn teuren Pferd zu Tod gehetzt!
Ja hat denn niemand von meiner Livree
dazwischen fahren mögen! Füttr' ich dafür
ein Schock baumlanger Lackeln, dass mir solche Schand'
passieren muss in meinem neucher Stadtpalais!

(going up to Octavian)

Hätt' wohl von Euer Liebden eines andern
Anstands mich verseh'n!

BARON
(groaning)

Oh! Oh!

FANINAL
(turning to the Baron)

Oh! Um das schöne freiherrliche Blut, was
auf den Boden rinnt!

(to Octavian)

O pfui! So eine ordinäre Metzgerei!

BARON

Hab' halt so ein jung und hitzig Blut,
Ist nicht zum Stillen! Oh!

FANINAL
(venting his anger on Octavian in restrained irony)

War mir von Euer Liebden hochgräflicher
Gegenwart allhier
wahrhaftig einer anderen Freud' gewärtig!

OCTAVIAN
(politely)

Er muss mich pardonieren.
Bin ausser Massen sehr betrübt über den Vorfall.
Bin aber ausser Schuld. Zu einer mehr gelegenen Zeit
erfahren Euer Liebden wohl den Hergang
aus Ihrer Fräulein Tochter Mund.

FANINAL
(controlling himself with difficulty)

Da möcht' ich recht sehr bitten!

SOPHIE
(determined)

Wie Sie befehlen, Vater. Werd' Ihnen Alles sagen.
Der Herr dort hat sich nicht so, wie er sollt'; betragen.

FANINAL
(angrily)

Ei, von wem red't Sie da? Von Ihrem Herrn Zukünft'gen?
Ich will nicht hoffen, wär' mir keine Manier.

SOPHIE
(quietly)

Ist nicht der Fall. Seh' ihn mit nichten an dafür.

95

FANINAL
(still more angrily)

Not give your hand?	Sieht ihn nicht an?

SOPHIE

No more. Look at me and forgive me, dear Papa!	Nicht mehr. Bitt' Sie dafür um gnädigen Pardon.

FANINAL
(first muttering to himself, then breaking out in fury)

Not give your hand! No more. Look and forgive.	Sieht ihn nicht an. Nicht mehr. Mich um Pardon.
Run through the body. By her side, that schoolboy.	Liegt dort gestochen. Steht bei ihr. Der Junge.

(breaking out)

How dare she! Broken the marriage of my dreams.	Blamage. Mir auseinander meine Eh'.
All the prying fools of the district and their jealous wives,	Alle Neidhammeln von der Wieden und der Leimgrub'n
How they will jeer! The surgeon! Quick! What if he dies here!	auf! in der Höh'! Der Medicus! Stirbt mir womöglich.

(to Sophie, beside himself with rage)

You marry him!	Sie heirat' ihn!

(The Doctor enters, and proceeds at once to attend to the Baron. Faninal turns to Octavian, changing his anger to obsequious civility out of respect for Rofrano's rank.)

And may I now, in all humility, request	Möcht' Euer Liebden recht in aller Devotion
Your Lordship to retire from my poor palace, fast as may be,	gebeten haben, schleunig sich von hier zu retirieren
And never more to show your face here!	und nimmer wieder zu erscheinen!

(to Sophie)

As for you!	Hör' Sie mich!
You marry him, and if he bleeds to death, no matter,	Sie heirat' ihn! Und wenn er sich verbluten tät,
Marry his lifeless body!	so heirat' Sie ihn als Toter!

The Doctor indicates with a reassuring gesture that the wounded man is in no danger. Octavian looks for his hat which had fallen under the servants' feet. A Maid hands it to him with a curtsey. Faninal makes an obeisance to Octavian, of exaggerated civility, but unmistakeable meaning. Octavian realizes that he cannot stay, but is longing to say one word more to Sophie; he answers Faninal's obeisance with an equally ceremonious bow. Faninal angrily bows a second, then a third time.

SOPHIE
(hurrying to speak the following words while Octavian is still within earshot. Curtseying)

Marry that man I will not living, and not dead!	Heirat' den Herrn dort nicht lebendig und nicht tot!
I will lock myself away in my room!	Sperr' mich zuvor in meine Kammer ein!

FANINAL
(bowing angrily to Octavian, who promptly returns the bow)

Ah! Lock yourself in! I've men enough	Ah! Sperrst dich ein. Sind Leut' genug im Haus,
To haul you to your carriage, Mistress Wilful.	die dich in Wagen tragen werden.

SOPHIE
(curtseying again)

I'll jump out from the carriage on my way to church.	Spring'aus dem Wagen noch, der mich zur Kirch'n führt!

FANINAL
(same business between himself and Octavian, who always moves a step nearer the door, but cannot tear himself away from Sophie)

Jump out from your carriage? Ha! I'll be at your side,	Ah! Springst noch aus dem Wagen! Na, ich sitz' neben dir,
And hold you till we get there.	und werd'dich schon halten!

SOPHIE
(curtseying again)

I promise I shall give the priest "No",	Geb' halt dem Pfarrer am Altar

| And not "Yes" for answer. | Nein anstatt Ja zur Antwort! |

(*In the meantime the Major-Domo dismisses the servants. The stage is gradually cleared. Only Lerchenau's servants remain with their Master.*)

FANINAL
(*same business*)

Ah! Give "No" and not "Yes" for an answer!	Ah! Gibst Nein anstatt Ja zur Antwort.
I'll shut you in a nunnery as I stand here!	Ich steck' dich in ein Kloster *stante pede*!
Go! Get you from my sight, Miss. Better now than next day!	Marsch! Mir aus meinen Augen! Lieber heut' als morgen!
For all your life!	Auf Lebenszeit!

SOPHIE
(*terrified*)

| I beg you to forgive me! I am not really bad! | Ich bitt' Sie um Pardon! Bin doch kein schlechtes Kind! |
| Forgive me, I pray you, for just this once! | Vergeben Sie mir nur dies eine Mal! |

FANINAL
(*furious, shutting his ears*)

| For all your life! For all your life! | Auf Lebenszeit! Auf Lebenszeit! |

OCTAVIAN
(*quickly, in an undertone*)

| Only be calm beloved, for my sake! | Sei Sie nur ruhig, Liebste, um Alles! |
| You'll hear from me! | Sie hört von mir! |

(*The Duenna pushes Octavian towards the door.*)

FANINAL

| For all your life! | Auf Lebenszeit! |

MARIANNE
(*drawing Sophie with her over to the right*)

| Go, hussy, get you from your father's presence! | So geh' [doch] nur dem Vater aus den Augen! |

(*She puts her through the door on the right and closes it. Octavian has left by the left-hand door. The Baron is surrounded by his servants, the Duenna, two maids, the Italians, and the Doctor. He is reclining on a couch made up from chairs, and now can be seen quite clearly.*)

FANINAL
(*shouting once more through the door by which Sophie left*)

| For all your life! | Auf Lebenszeit! |

(*hurrying over to the Baron*)

| I kiss your hand, Sir. I must embrace you, my dear Baron! | Bin überglücklich! Muss Euer Liebden embrassieren! |

BARON
(*hurt in the arm by the embrace*)

| Oh! Oh! Jesus Maria! | Oh! Oh! Jesus Maria! |

FANINAL
(*to the right, his rage increasing again*)

| Jezebel! To a nunnery! | Luderei! In's Kloster! |

(*towards the centre door*)

| Into prison! | Ein Gefängnis! |
| For all your life! | Auf Lebenszeit! |

BARON

| All right! All right! A drop of something liquid. | Is gut! Is gut! Ein Schluck von was zu trinken! |

FANINAL

| Some wine? Some beer? Some hippocras with ginger? | Ein Wein? Ein Bier! Ein Hippokras mit Ingwer? |

(*The Doctor makes a nervous, deprecating gesture; Faninal continues, lamenting*)

Breeding and birth! So noble in misfortune!	So einen Herrn Zurichten miserabel!
And in my palace too! You'll marry him, so much the sooner!	In meinem Stadtpalais! Sie heirat' ihn um desto früher!
I'm master here!	Bin Mann's genug!

BARON
(wearily)

All right, all right!	Is gut, is gut!

FANINAL
(towards the left-hand door, his anger flaring up again)

I'm master here!	Bin Mann's genug!

(to the Baron)

I kiss your hand for such polite indulgence.	Küss' Ihm die Hand für Seine Güt' und Nachsicht.
We are yours to command–I'll run and bring you–	Gehört all's Ihm im Haus. Ich lauf'–und bring' Ihm–

(to the right)

A nunnery is too good!	Ein Kloster ist zu gut!

(to the Baron)

Be at your ease.	Sei'n ausser Sorg'.

(very obsequiously)

I know what satisfaction is due from me.	Weiss, was ich Satisfaction Ihm schuldig bin.

(He rushes off. The Duenna and the Maids leave at the same time. The two Italians have slunk off during the preceding action. The Baron is left alone with his servants and the Doctor. Soon a footman comes with a carafe of wine, and offers it to the Baron.)

BARON
(sitting up slightly)

Well, here I am. What accidents befall a man of quality	Da lieg' ich. Was ei'm Cavalier nit all's passieren kann
In this old Vienna town.	in dieser Wienerstadt!
It does not suit me here. We're much too clearly in the hands of God.	Wär' nicht mein Gusto hier,–da is ein's gar zu sehr in Gottes Hand,
I'd rather be at home!	wär' lieber daheim!

(He tries to drink and makes a movement which hurts.)

Oh! Oh! The devil! Oh! Oh! A plague upon that boy!	Oh! Oh! Der Satan! Oh! Oh! Sakraments- verfluchter Bub'!
Not dry yet behind the ears, and plays with swords already.	Nit trocken hinter'm Ohr und fuchtelt mit'n Spadi!

(with increasing anger)

Insolent scurvy dog! Wait, wait until I catch you. I'll kill you.	Wällischer Hundsbub' das! Dich sollt, ich nur erwischen,
I swear I'll throw you in with the dogs to cool your heels.	in Hundezwinger sperr' ich dich ein bei meiner Seel'.
In the chicken-coop, no, no, the pigsty.	In Hühnerstall! In Schweinekofen!
That's where I'll put you! I'll make you hear the angels sing!	Tät dich kuranzen! Solltest alle Engel singen hör'n!

LERCHENAU'S SERVANTS
(At once assuming a very dangerous and threatening attitude, turning to the door by which Octavian left.)

We will do for you,	Wenn ich dich erwisch
Beat you black and blue,	Du liegst unter'm Tisch.
Wait, our time will come,	Wart', dich richt' ich zu,
Vile Italian scum!	Wällischer Filou!

BARON
(to Faninal's footman who is waiting on him)

Give me some more wine, quick!	Schenk' Er nur ein da, schnell!

(The Doctor pours it out for the Baron and gives it to him. As he drinks his humour gradually returns.)

I can't help laughing, just to think [12] what fancies	Und doch, muss lachen, wie sich so ein Loder
A boy like that can have, he gives himself such airs:	mit seine siebzehn Jahr' die Welt imaginiert:
Seems to think he can arrange my affairs.	meint, Gott weiss wie er mich contre- veniert.
Haha! Well, we'll see who laughs the longest! Not for worlds, though,	Haha! umgekehrt ist auch gefahren! Möcht' um alles nicht,
Would I have missed the chance to see [33] that saucy baggage spitting fire at me!	dass ich dem Mädel sein rebellisch Aufbegehren nicht verspüret hätt'!

98

There's nothing I know that excites me so much,	Gibt auf der Welt nichts was mich enflammiert
Or that renews my youth so well, as a defiant wench!	und also vehement verjüngt als wie ein rechter Trotz!

LERCHENAU'S SERVANTS
(in hollow voices)

We will do for you,	Wart', dich hau i z'samm,
Vile Italian cur,	Wällischer Filou,
We will do for you,	Wart', dich hau i z'samm,
Beat him black and blue!	dass dich Gott verdamm'!

BARON
(turning to the Doctor)

Herr Medicus, you go now to my room!	Herr Medicus, verfüg' Er sich voraus!
And make my bed, of softest feather bedding!	Mach' Er das Bett aus lauter Federbetten.
I'll come, but first I'll have more wine. Now off with you, good doctor.	Ich komm'. Erst aber trink' ich noch. Marschier' Er nur indessen.

(He empties the second cup. Annina has entered through the ante-room, and approaches him discreetly, a letter in her hand. Quietly, to himself.)

A feather bed. Two hours before we eat. I'll die of boredom.	Ein Federbett. Zwei Stunden noch zu Tisch. Werd' zeitlang haben.
"Without me, without me, every day [31] is so long.	"Ohne mich, ohne mich, jeder Tag dir so bang;
With me, with me, never night is too long".	"Mit mir, mit mir, keine Nacht dir zu lang".

(Annina places herself so that the Baron cannot avoid seeing her, and makes mysterious signs with the letter.)

For me?	Für mich?

ANNINA
(approaching)

From one you know of.	Von der Bewussten.

BARON

And who, pray, may that be?	Wer soll da [mit] gemeint sein?

ANNINA
(coming quite close to him)

To your hands only, and in secret can I give it.	Nur eigenhändig, insgeheim zu übergeben.

BARON

Room there!	Luft da!

(His servants retire, unceremoniously taking the carafe from Faninal's Footman and emptying it.)

Show me the thing!	Zeig' Sie den Wisch!

(He opens the letter with his left hand, tries to read it, holding it far from his eyes.)

Look for my glasses here in my pocket.	Such' Sie in meiner Tasche meine Brillen.

(very suspiciously, as she is searching)

No! Better not. If you can read, let's hear it.	Nein! Such' Sie nicht! Kann Sie geschrieb'nes lesen?
There!	Da.

ANNINA
(taking it and reading it)

"Herr Cavalier! Tomorrow come evening I'll be free.	"Herr Cavalier! Den morgigen Abend hätt' i frei.
I liked you at once, but I	"Sie ham mir schon g'fall'n nur g'schamt
Was too shy there before Her Highness,	"hab i mi vor der fürstli'n Gnadn,
'Cos I am only a young girl. Your most loving Mariandl,	"weil i noch gar so jung bin. Das bewusste Mariandl,
Humble serving girl and sweetheart.	"Kammerzofel und Verliebte.
Hoping Herr Cavalier has not completely forgotten me.	"Wenn der Herr Cavalier den Namen nit schon vergessen hat.
I wait an answer."	"I wart' auf Antwort."

BARON
(delighted)

She waits an answer.	Sie wart' auf Antwort.

99

It all goes so well, just like home,
There is though quite a different style in town.

(very merry)

I still have all the luck of the Lerchenaus.

Come back tonight, I'll give the answer and in writing.

ANNINA

Yours to command, Herr Cavalier. You won't forget your servant?

BARON
(not hearing)

"Without me, without me, every day is too long".

ANNINA
(more insistently)

You won't forget your servant, Your Highness?

BARON

All right.
"With me, with me, not a night is too long."

(Annina makes another begging gesture.)

BARON

Later on. All in good time. Don't forget

She waits an answer. Leave me now a moment.
Go to my room, get me my pen and ink, and I will
Think of an answer to dictate!

(Exit Annina, not without indicating with a threatening gesture behind the Baron's back that she will soon be even with him for his niggardliness. The Baron takes a last sip of wine.)

"With me, with me, not a night is too long!"

Geht all's recht am Schnürl so wie z'Haus und hat noch einen andern Schick dazu.

Ich hab' halt schon einmal ein lerchenauisch' Glück.

Komm' Sie nach Tisch, geb' ihr die Antwort nachher schriftlich.

Ganz zu Befehl, Herr Cavalier, Vergessen nicht der Botin?

"Ohne mich, ohne mich, jeder Tag dir so bang".

Vergessen nicht der Botin, Euer Gnad'n?

Schon gut.
"Mit mir, mit mir, keine Nacht dir zu lang."

Das später. All's auf einmal. Dann zum Schluss.

Sie wart' auf Antwort! Tret' Sie ab indessen.
Schaff' Sie ein Schreibzeug in mein Zimmer hin, dort drüben,
dass ich die Antwort dann diktier.

"Mit mir, mit mir, keine Nacht dir zu lang!"

Exit slowly, and quite at his ease, accompanied by his servants.

Curtain.

100

Act Three

Introduction and Pantomime. A private room in an inn. At the back, to the left, a recess, with a bed in it. The recess separated from the room by a curtain, which can be drawn. In the centre, towards the left, a fire-place, with a fire; over it a mirror. In front on the left a door leading to a side room. Opposite the fire-place is a table laid for two, on which stands a large, many-branched candlestick. At the back, in the centre, a door leading to the corridor. Next to it on the right, a sideboard. Right back, a blind window; in front, on the right, a window looking onto the street. Candelabra with candles on the sideboard and on the chimney-piece, and sconces on the walls. Only one candle is burning in each candlestick on the chimney-piece. The room is in semi-darkness. Annina discovered, dressed as a lady in mourning. Valzacchi is arranging her veil, putting her dress to rights, takes a step backwards, surveys her, takes a crayon from his pocket and paints her eyes.

The door on the left is opened cautiously, a head appears, and then vanishes. Then a not unsuspicious-looking, but decently dressed, old woman slips in, opens the door silently, and respectfully introduces Octavian, in female clothes, with a cap, such as girls of the middle-classes wear. Octavian, followed by the old woman, moves towards the two others. Valzacchi is at once aware of him, stops what he is doing, and bows to Octavian. Annina does not at once recognize him in his disguise. She cannot restrain her astonishment, and curtsies low. Octavian feels in his pocket (not like a woman, but like a man, and one sees that under his skirt he is wearing riding-boots and spurs) and throws a purse to Valzacchi. Valzacchi and Annina kiss his hand. Annina puts a finishing touch to his kerchief. Five suspicious-looking men enter, very cautiously, from the left. Valzacchi makes a sign to them to wait. They stand at the left, near the door. A clock strikes the half-hour. Valzacchi takes out his watch, shows it to Octavian: it is high time. Octavian hurries out to the left, followed by the old woman, who acts as his duenna. Valzacchi leads the suspicious-looking men to the front, impressing on them with every gesture the necessity of extreme caution. They follow him on tiptoe to the centre. Annina goes to the mirror (all the while carefully avoiding making a noise) completes her disguise; then draws from a pocket a piece of paper, from which she seems to be learning a part. Valzacchi signals to one of the suspicious-looking men to follow him noiselessly, quite noiselessly. He leads him to the wall on the right, noiselessly opens a trap-door, not far from the table, makes the man descend, closes the trapdoor again, then summons two others to his side, slinks in front of them to the door of the room, puts his head out, assures himself that they are unobserved, makes a sign to them to appear to him, and lets them out. Then he closes the door, directs the two remaining men to precede him silently to the door leading to the side-room, and pushes them out. He beckons to Annina to come to him, goes out with her silently, noiselessly closes the door behind him, and then returns. He claps his hands. The man who is hidden rises to his waist from the trap-door. At the same moment heads appear above the bed and in other places. At a sign from Valzacchi they disappear as suddenly–the secret panels close without a sound. [36]

Valzacchi looks again at his watch, goes to the back, opens the door. Then he produces a tinder-box and busily lights the candles on the table. A waiter and a boy run in with tapers for lighting candles. They light the candles on the chimney, on the side-board, and the numerous sconces. They have left the door open behind them; dance music is heard from the ante-room at the back. [16, 37, 38, 39]

Valzacchi hurries to the centre doors, opens them both respectfully, and bowing low steps aside.

Baron Ochs appears, his arm in a sling, leading Octavian by his left, followed by his Body Servant. The Baron surveys the room. Octavian looks around, runs to the mirror, arranges his hair. The Baron notices the Waiter and the Boy who are about to light more candles, and signals to them to stop. In their preoccupation they do not notice him. The Baron impatiently pulls the Boy from the chair onto which he had climbed, and extinguishes some of the candles nearest him with his hand. Valzacchi discreetly points out the recess to him and, by opening the curtains, the bed.

The Landlord hurries forward with several waiters to greet their noble guest.

LANDLORD

What can my poor house still offer Your Lordship?	Haben Euer Gnaden noch weit're Befehle;

FOUR WAITERS

A few more candles?	Befehl'n mehr Lichter?

LANDLORD

A better apartment?	Ein grösseres Zimmer?

101

A few more candles for My Lord?	Befehl'n mehr Lichterauf dem Tisch?
More silver?	Mehr Silber?

BARON

(*busily occupied with a napkin which he has taken from the table and is using to extinguish all the candles which he can reach*)

Be off! Or you will give the girl ideas!	Verschwindt's! Macht mir das Mädel net verrückt!
Who asked for music? Didn't order that.	Was will die Musik? Hab' sie nicht bestellt.

(*putting out more candles*)

LANDLORD

Shall they be told to come and play in here?	Schaffen vielleicht, dass man sie näher hört?
And while you dine they'll play some music.	Im Vorsaal da is Tafelmusik?

BARON

Leave your damned fiddlers where they are.	Lass Er die Musik, wo sie ist.

(*noticing the blind window on the right behind the table*)

What is that little window there?	Was is da für ein Fenster da?

(*trying to open it*)

LANDLORD

'Tis only sham, My Lord.	Ein blindes Fenster nur.

(*bows*)

Your Lordship's supper waits.	Darf aufgetragen werd'n?

(*All five waiters make as if to hurry off.*)

BARON

Stop! What do these black beetles want?	Halt, was woll'n die Maikäfer da?

WAITERS

(*at the door*)

We wait on Your Lordship.	Servier'n, Euer Gnaden.

BARON

(*making a sign for them to go*)

I don't need help.	Brauch' niemand nicht.

(*when they hesitate; roughly*)

Off now! My servant shall do all the serving here:	Packt's Euch! Servieren wird mein Kammerdiener da,
And I can pour the wine out. D'you hear me?	Einschenken tu'ich selber. Versteht Er?

(*Valzacchi signals to them to respect His Lordship's wish without demur. He pushes them all out of the door. The Baron begins again to extinguish a number of candles, among them some high on the wall, which he can only reach with difficulty; to Valzacchi*)

You are a worthy fellow. If you can get the bill reduced a little,	Er ist ein braver Kerl. Wenn Er mir hilft, die Rechnung runterdrucken,
Something will come your way. I'm sure it costs a fortune here.	Dann fällt was ab für Ihn. Kost'sicher hier ein Martergeld.

(*Exit Valzacchi, bowing low. Octavian has now finished. The Baron leads him to a table, they sit down. The Body Servant by the sideboard contemplates the development of the tête-à-tête with insolent curiosity. He places bottles of wine from the sideboard on the table. The Baron pours out wine. Octavian sips. The Baron kisses Octavian's hand. Octavian withdraws his hand. The Baron signals to the lackey to withdraw, but has to repeat the signal several times before he goes.*)

OCTAVIAN

(*pushing back his glass*)

No, no, let be! No wine for me.	[40] Nein, nein, nein, nein! I trink kein Wein.

BARON

Why sweetheart, what next? Come, don't be so bashful.	Geh, Herzerl, was denn? Mach' doch keine Faxen.

OCTAVIAN

No, no, no, no, I must not stay.	Nein, nein, i bleib net da.

(*He jumps up as if he was about to go.*)

BARON

(*seizing him with his left hand*)

You drive me to despair.	Sie macht mich deschparat.

OCTAVIAN

I know, Sir, what you think. Oh, you naughty man!	Ich weiss schon, was Sie glaub'n. Oh Sie schlimmer Herr!

BARON
(very loud)

Lord strike me pink! I swear by all my patron saints! | Saperdipix! Ich schwör bei meinem Schutzpatron!

OCTAVIAN

(feigns great terror; he runs–as if by mistake–instead of to the door, into the recess, tears the curtains apart, and sees the bed. He pretends to be utterly astonished, and returns in consternation on tiptoe.)

Jesus Maria, there's a bed there, a bloody great big one. | Jesus Maria, steht a Bett drin, a mordsmässig grosses.
Lor' bless me, who's it for? | Ja mei, wer schlaft denn da?

BARON
(leading him back to the table)

You'll know in good time. Just come now. Sit down with me. | Das wird Sie schon seh'n. Jetzt komm' Sie. Setz' Sie sich schön.
They'll soon bring us our supper. Something wrong with your appetite? | Kommt gleich wer mit'n Essen. Hat Sie denn kein' Hunger nicht?

(Puts his arm around his waist.)

OCTAVIAN
(casting languishing looks at the Baron)

O Lord! What a way for a bride-groom to act. | O weh, wo Sie [ja] doch ein Bräutgam tun sein.

(pushes him off)

BARON

Oh, can't you for once leave that word alone. | Ach lass Sie schon einmal das fade Wort!
You sit here with a cavalier at your side, | Sie hat doch einen Kavalier vor sich
Not with some lout of a footman: | und keinen Seifensieder:
A cavalier leaves all | Ein Kavalier lässt alles,
That is not quite to his taste | was ihm nicht konveniert,
Outside there by the door. Here sits no bridegroom | da draussen vor der Tür. Hier sitzt kein Bräutigam
Nor any lady's chambermaid: | und keine Kammerjungfer nicht;
Here sits at supper a man in love and with the girl who stole his heart. | Hier sitzt mit seiner Allerschönsten ein Verliebter beim Souper.

(He draws Octavian nearer to him, who leans back coquettishly in his chair, with half-closed eyes. Then he rises. The moment for the first kiss seems to have come. As his face comes close to his companion's, he is violently struck by the likeness to Octavian. He starts backwards, and unconsciously feels his wounded arm.)

That face again! That blasted boy! | Ist *ein* Gesicht! Verfluchter Bub!
His face pursues me waking and in dreams! | Verfolgt mich also wacher und im Traum!

[41, 42]

OCTAVIAN
(opening his eyes and looking at him with impudent coquetry)

What do you mean? | Was meint Er denn?

BARON

Your face reminds me of a godforsaken boy! | Sieht einem ähnlich, einem gottverfluchten Kerl!

OCTAVIAN

Go on! I never heard of such stuff! | Ah geh! Das hab i no net g'hört!

(The Baron once again quite certain that it is the chamber-maid, forces a smile. But he is not quite free of fear; he has to breathe deeply, and so the kiss is postponed. The man under the trap-door opens it too soon and appears. [36] Octavian, who is sitting opposite him, makes violent signs to him to get out of sight. He vanishes at once. The Baron, taking a few steps to shake off the unpleasant impression, and about to embrace Octavian from behind, catches a last glimpse of him. He is violently alarmed and points to the spot. Octavian continues as if he did not understand.)

What's wrong with you? | Was ist mit Ihm?

BARON
(pointing to the spot where the apparition vanished)

Lord, what was that? Didn't you see something there? | Was war denn das? Hat Sie den nicht geseh'n?

Never a thing.   Da is ja nix.

Not a thing?   Da is nix?
                    (*again anxiously scanning Octavian's face*)
No?   So?
Nothing there neither?   Und da is auch nix?
                    (*He passes his hand over his face.*)

Why, that's my face.   Da is mei G'sicht.

                    (*breathing heavily, pouring out a glass of wine*)
This is your face–and nothing there–I think   Da is Ihr G'sicht–und da is nix–mir scheint,
My head is going to burst.   ich hab' die Congestion.
(*He falls heavily into a chair. He is ill at ease. The door is opened, and the music outside can be
heard again.* [31] *The Body Servant comes in and serves.*)

                    (*very sentimentally*)
What lovely music!   Die schöne Musik!

                    (*very loud again*)
It's my favourite song, you know.   Is mei Lieblied, weiss Sie das?

                    (*listening to the music*)
It makes me weepy.   Da muss ma weinen.

What?   Was?

'Cos it's so pretty.   Weils gar so schön is.

What, weeping? Don't be sad.   Was, weinen? Wär' nicht schlecht.
You must enjoy yourself, the music fires the   Kreuzlustig muss Sie sein, die Musik geht
  blood.   in's Blut.
                    (*sentimentally*)
Is it clear   G'spürt Sie's jetzt
                    (*signalling to the servant to go*)
Now, my dear? Do you not see   Auf die letzt, g'spürt Sie's dahier,
How it is with me?   Dass Sie aus mir,
You now can make of me your willing   Kann machen alles frei, was Sie nur will.
  slave.
(*The Servant opens the door again, looks in with insolent curiosity, and does not go till the
Baron has made an angry sign.*)

                    (*leaning back, as if speaking to himself, with exaggerated melancholy*)
'Tis all one, 'tis all one, 'tis all one,   [43] Es is ja eh als eins, es is ja eh als eins–
  'tis all one–
All our joys, all our bitter pain.   Was ein Herz [auch] noch so gach begehrt.
                    (*as the Baron takes his hand*)
In the end are they not all in vain?   Geh' es is ja all's net drumi wert.

                    (*letting go of his hand*)
Why, what's this? Oh, they're not all in   Ei was denn? Is sehr wohl der Müh' wert!
  vain.

                    (*still just as melancholy, casting smouldering glances at the Baron*)
As the hours do fly, as the wind blows by,   Wie die Stund' hingeht, wie der Wind
                                                    verweht,
So must we too shortly pass away.   So sind wir bald alle zwei dahin.
'Tis the lot of man,   Menschen sin' ma halt,
                    (*languishing glance at the Baron*)
            that we nothing can.   richtn's nicht mit Gewalt,
Not an eye shall weep, nor for your loss,   Weint uns Niemand nach, net dir net und
  nor for mine.   net mir.

Is it the wine that makes you so sad?	Macht Sie der Wein leicht immer so?
It must be your corset cramps your poor little heart.	Is ganz gewiss' Ihr Mieder, das auf's Herzer [Ihr] druckt.

(*Octavian with closed eyes, gives no answer.*)

BARON

(*rises and tries to undo his dress*)

I must say I am feeling warm.	Jetzt wird's frei mir a bisserl heiss.

(*Without ado he takes off his wig, looking for a place to put it. At that moment he catches a glimpse of a face which appears in the recess and stares at him. The face vanishes in a trice. He says "Brainstorm" to himself, and struggles with his fear, but has to mop his forehead. His eyes again fall on the chambermaid, slumped helplessly on the chair. He is overcome by this, and approaches tenderly. Then he again seems to see Octavian's face close to his own. He starts back again. Mariandl hardly stirs. Once more the Baron wrestles with his fear, forcing himself to put a cheerful face on it. Then his eyes again alight on a strange face, staring at him from the wall. Now he is beside himself with terror: he gives a muffled scream, seizes the hand-bell from the table and rings it distractedly.*)

There, and there, and there, and there!	Da und da und da und da!

(*Suddenly the supposedly blind window is torn open, Annina in mourning appears, and points with outstretched arms to the Baron, who is distraught with fear.*)

There and there, and there, and there!	Da und da und da und da!

(*He tries to protect his back.*)

ANNINA

My husband! Yes, it is he! 'Tis he!	Er ist es! Es ist mein Mann! Er ist's.

(*She vanishes.*)

BARON

(*alarmed*)

Lord, what was that?	Was ist denn das?

OCTAVIAN

This place is all bewitched.	Das Zimmer is verhext.

(*crosses himself*)

ANNINA

(*followed by Valzacchi, who makes a pretence of holding her back, rushes in by the centre door, with the Landlord and Three Waiters. Speaking with a Bohemian accent, but in educated tones*)

I am his wife! I'll get my hands on him,	Es ist mein Mann, ich leg' Beschlag auf ihn!
God is my witness. You be witness also!	Gott ist mein Zeuge, Sie sind meine Zeugen!
The law, and the government, Her Majesty,	Gerichte! Hohe Obrigkeit! Die Kaiserin
Give me back my beloved!	muss ihn mir wiedergeben!

BARON

(*to the Landlord*)

What does this woman want of me, you fool!	Was will das Weibsbild da von mir, Herr Wirt!
What does he want, and he, and he, and he?	Was will der dort und der und der und der?

(*pointing all round the room*)

The devil has his home in your God-forsaken third-rate coffee-house.	Der Teufel frequentier' Sein gottver-fluchtes Extrazimmer!

ANNINA

And would you dare deny me, villain!	Er wagt mich zu verleugnen, ah!
And make pretence you do not know me?	[Er] tut, als ob er mich nicht täte kennen!

BARON

(*He has put a cold compress on his head, holds it in its place with his left hand, then goes right up to the Landlord, the Waiters, and Annina in turn, scanning them closely, as if to convince himself that they are real.*)

Alive, by Heaven!	Is auch lebendig!

(*He throws the compress away. Very emphatically*)

This baggage, I protest, I never saw before!	Ich hab' wahrhaftigen Gott das Möbel nie gesehn!

(*to the Landlord*)

Begone now, all of you, and let us sup in peace!	Debarassier' Er mich und lass' Er fort servier'n!
I vow I'll never more set foot in your low pot-house.	Ich hab' Sein Beisl heut' zum letzten Mal betreten!

ANNINA
(as if only now noticing Octavian's presence)

Ah! It is true, what all my friends did tell me,	Ah! Es ist wahr, was mir berichtet wurde,
That he intends a second marriage, oh the monster,	Er will ein zweitesmal heiraten, der Infame,
A second innocent maiden such as I once was.	Ein zweites unschuldiges Mädchen so wie ich es war!

(The Landlord is alarmed.)

THREE WAITERS

Oh! Your Lordship!	Oh, Euer Gnaden!

BARON

What, am I in a madhouse? Plague on you all!	Bin ich in einem Narrnturm? Kreuzelement!

(He shakes Valzacchi who is standing next to him, violently.)

Am I Baron Ochs of Lerchenau, tell me, or am I not?	Bin ich der Baron [von] Lerchenau oder bin ich es nicht?
Am I possessed?	Bin ich bei mir?

(holding a finger in a candle)

Is that a candle,	Is' das ein Kerzl,

(brandishing a napkin)

And is that a napkin?	Is das ein Serviettl?

ANNINA

Yes, yes, you are he, and as true as you are he,	Ja, ja du bist es und so wahr als du es bist,
I am your wife, and you know me full well.	Bin ich es auch und du erkennst mich wohl,
Leupold, reflect:	Leupold bedenk':
Leupold Anton von Lerchenau, above us all dwells a judge that knoweth all!	Leupold Anton von Lerchenau, dort oben richtet dich ein Höherer!

(At first he starts violently, so that her speech is interrupted, but she quickly regains her composure.)

BARON
(staring at her in bewilderment)

Surely I know you.	Kommt mir bekannt vor.

(looking at Octavian again)

They all have double faces, all of them together.	Hab'n doppelte Gesichter alle mit einander.

LANDLORD

Poor ill-used lady, wretched, ill-used lady.	Die arme Frau Baronin!

(Four Children between the ages of four and ten rush in, too early, and make for the Baron.)

FOUR CHILDREN

Papa! Papa! Papa!	Papa! Papa! Papa!

ANNINA

Hear you the voices of your offspring?	Hörst du die Stimme deines Blutes?
Children, raise your hands to him in prayer!	Kinder, hebt Eure Hände auf zu ihm!

BARON
(angrily hitting out at the four children with a napkin which he has seized from the table; to the Landlord.)

Take all this crew away from here at once.	Debarassier' Er mich von Denen da,
Take her, take him, and him, and him!	Von der, von dem, von dem, von dem!

(pointing in all directions. Valzacchi meanwhile talks quietly to Octavian.

OCTAVIAN
(to Valzacchi)

Have messengers been sent for Faninal yet?	Ist gleich wer fort, den Faninal zu holen?

VALZACCHI
(whispering)

Ere you 'ad come 'ere. In a moment 'e is 'ere.	Sogleich in Anfang. Wird sogleich zur Stelle sein.

(*whispering behind the Baron's back*)

Asking your pardon, go not too far,	Halten zu Gnaden, geh'n nit zu weit,
Else it might end in harm for you, harm most serious!	Könnten recht böse Folgen g'spür'n! Bitterböse!

BARON

What? Harm to me from that beldam there?	Was? ich was g'spür'n? von dem Möbel da?
Ne'er have I touched her, not with a pitchfork's end!	Hab's nie nicht angerührt, nicht mit der Feuerzang'!

ANNINA
(*screaming shrilly*)

Aah!	Aah!

LANDLORD
(*as before*)

For bigamy is not a trifle,	Die Bigamie ist halt kein G'spass,
It is a hanging matter.	Is [halt] ein kapital Verbrechen!

VALZACCHI
(*softly, to the Baron*)

I counsel Your Lordship to 'ave a care.	Ik rat Euer Gnaden, sei'n vorsiktig,
Ze police in zis town, it 'ave no mercy, Sir!	Die Sittenpolizei sein gar nicht tolerant!

BARON

Bigamy? Pooh! A fig for your police!	Die Bigamie? Die Sittenpolizei?

(*mimicking the children's voices*)

Papa, Papa, Papa?	Papa, Papa, Papa?

(*striking his head as if in despair, then furiously*)

Throw out that screaming Jezebel!	Schmeiss 'Er hinaus das Trauerpferd!
Who? What? You will not!	Wer? Was? Er will nicht?
What? The police! Won't they do anything? Are the whole lot of you	Was? Polizei! Die Lack'ln woll'n nicht? Spielt das Gelichter
Only a pack of cowards?	Leicht Alls unter einem Leder?
Are we in Paris? Or a cannibal island?	Sein wir in Frankreich? Sein wir unter [die] Kurutzen?
Or in Her Majesty's own city?	Oder in kaiserlicher Hauptstadt?

(*He pulls open the window looking onto the street.*)

Hey police!	Polizei!
Police there, hey, Police! I call you here to help me.	Herauf da, Polizei! Gilt Ordnung herzustellen
I am a nobleman, my life's in danger.	Und einer Stand'sperson zu Hilf' zu eilen!

(*Loud cries of Police are heard from the street.*)

LANDLORD
(*lamenting*)

Oh! My old inn disgraced	Mein renommiertes Haus!
And my good reputation.	Das muss mein Haus erleben!

CHILDREN
(*whining*)

Papa! Papa! Papa!	Papa! Papa! Papa!

(*Enter the Commissar of Police with Two Constables of the Watch. All stand back to make room for them.*)

VALZACCHI
(*to Octavian*)

O Dio! What can we do?	Oh weh, was maken wir?

OCTAVIAN

Have confidence in me and leave the rest to chance.	Verlass' Er sich auf mich und lass' Er's geh'n wie's geht.

VALZACCHI

Your 'umble servant to command!	Zu Euer Excellenz Befehl!

COMMISSAR
(*roughly*)

Halt! Keep your places! What is wrong?	Halt! Keiner rührt sich! Was ist los?
Who was it called for help? Who was it broke the peace?	Wer hat um Hilf' geschrie'n? Wer hat Skandal gemacht?

BARON

(going towards him with the self-confidence of a great gentleman)

It's all in order now. I am happy to see you. — Is all's in Ordnung jetzt. Bin mit Ihm wohl zufrieden.

I always knew that in Vienna there's no danger. — Hab' gleich verhofft, dass in Wien all's [recht] wie am Schnürl geht.

(cheerfully)

Drive all the riffraff away, I wish to dine in private. — Schaff' Er das Pack mir da vom Hals. Ich will in Ruh' soupieren.

COMMISSAR

And who are you? — Wer ist der Herr? Was gibt dem Herrn
What right have you to intervene? — Befugnis?
Is this your house? — Ist Er der Wirt?

(The Baron gapes; the Commissar continues brusquely.)

Then keep a civil tongue and wait a moment, — Dann halt Er sich gefällig still
Till I come to question you. — Und wart' Er bis man Ihn vernehmen wird.

(The Baron retires in perplexity, begins to look for his wig, which has disappeared in the confusion, and cannot be found. The Commissar sits down; the two Constables take up their position behind him.)

Who is in charge? — Wo ist der Wirt?

LANDLORD

(submissively)

Pray let me, excellent Sir Constable, only speak for myself, Sir. — Mich dem Herrn Oberkommissarius schönstens zu rekommandieren.

COMMISSAR

Your premises do not speak well for you. — Die Wirtschaft da rekommandiert Ihn schlecht,
Now, your report. The whole truth! — Bericht Er jetzt! Von Anfang!

LANDLORD

Herr Kommissar! His Lordship here— — Herr Kommissar! Der Herr Baron—

COMMISSAR

That great big fat man there? Where have you put your wig, Sir? — Der grosse Dicke da? Wo hat Er sein Päruckl?

BARON

(who has been looking for it all this time)

That's what I'm asking you! — [Um] Das frag' ich Ihn!

LANDLORD

That is my Lord, the Baron Lerchenau! — Das ist der Herr Baron von Lerchenau!

COMMISSAR

Then prove it. — Genügt nicht.

BARON

What? — Was?

COMMISSAR

Is there a man of standing here — Hat Er Personen nahebei,
Whom you can call as witness? — Die für Ihn Zeugnis geben?

BARON

Right here at hand. There, my secretary, that Italian. — Gleich bei der Hand! Da hier mein Sekretär, ein Italiener.

VALZACCHI

(exchanging a glance of understanding with Octavian)

I do not know this gentleman. He may Be a Baron, he may be not. I do not know. — Ik excusier mik. Ik weiss nix. Die Herr kann sein Baron, kann sein auch nit. Ik weiss von nix.

BARON

(beside himself)

That's the last straw, you dirty, lying scoundrel! — Das ist doch stark, wällischer Bruder, falscher!

(The Baron approaches him with his left hand raised.)

108

COMMISSAR
(sharply, to the Baron)

You'd better keep a civil tongue.	Für's erste moderier' Er sich.

OCTAVIAN
(Having stood quietly on the right up till now, runs back and forth as if in despair, unable to find the way out, and mistakes the window for the door.)

Oh my God, could I sink through the floor now!	Oh mein Gott, in die Erd'n möcht'ich sinken!
Oh Holy Mother of God, you must help me!	Heilige Mutter von Maria Taferl!

COMMISSAR

That young person there, who is she?	Wer ist dort die junge Person?

BARON

She? No-one. She stands under my protection here.	Die? Niemand. Sie steht unter meiner Protection!

COMMISSAR

Yourself will soon find some protection very necessary.	Er selber wird bald eine Protection sehr nötig haben.
Who is the little wench, why is she here?	Wer ist das junge Ding, was macht sie hier?

(looking around)

I have suspicion that you are one of those abandoned men who lead	Ich will nicht hoffen, dass Er ein gottverdammter Debauchierer
Young girls astray! It would go hard with you.	und Verführer ist! Da könnt's Ihm schlecht ergeh'n.
Once more, how come you by her? Answer quickly.	Wie kommt Er zu dem Mädel? Antwort will ich.

OCTAVIAN

Farewell. The river.	I geh ins Wasser!

(Octavian runs towards the recess as though to escape, and tears open the curtain, disclosing the peacefully illuminated bed.)

COMMISSAR
(rising)

What's this, Landlord, what's this?	Herr Wirt, was seh' ich da?
What business do you carry on?	Was für ein Handwerk treibt denn Er?

LANDLORD
(confused)

When there are persons of rank and fashion–come to dine or sup–	Wenn ich Personen von Stand zum speisen oder Nachtmahl hab'–

COMMISSAR

Hold you your tongue: wait till I question you.	Halt' Er den Mund. Ich nehm' Ihn später vor.

(to the Baron)

Now I will count to three, then you must tell me	Jetzt zähl' ich noch bis drei, dann will ich wissen,
How it comes that this honest girl is here with you.	Wie Er da zu dem jungen Bürgermädchen kommt!
And I would have you know you had better not deceive me with lying answers.	Ich will nicht hoffen, dass Er sich einer falschen Aussag' wird unterfangen.

(The Landlord and Valzacchi indicate with gestures to the Baron how dangerous the situation is and how important his statement is.)

BARON
(signalling confidently to them that they may rely on him, and that he was not born yesterday)

The Captain of the Watch, for sure, will think no harm	Wird wohl kein Anstand sein bei Ihm, Herr Kommissar,
If men of quality with their affianced brides	Wenn eine Standsperson mit seiner ihm verlobten Braut
Should choose to sit at supper at nine o'clock here in this inn.	Um neune abends ein Souper einnehmen tut.

(He glances around him to see the effect of his explanation.)

COMMISSAR

She your affianced bride? Then state her father's name	Das wäre Seine Braut? Geb' Er den Namen an
And tell me where he lives. And if you've	Vom Vater und's Logis. Wenn Seine

spoke the truth,	Angab' stimmt
You'll be free with the girl at once to leave us.	Mag Er sich mit der Jungfer retirieren.

BARON

Pray, do you know to whom you speak? I'm not accustomed–	Ich bin wahrhaftig nicht gewohnt, in dieser Weise–

COMMISSAR
(sharply)

Answer without ado, else I will sing quite another tune.	Mach' Er Seine Aussag' oder ich zieh' andere Seiten auf.

BARON

All right, I'll tell you. This is Fräulein Faninal,	Werd' nicht mankieren. Ist die Jungfer Faninal,
Sophie Anna Barbara, daughter to that	Sophia Anna Barbara, ehliche Tochter
Most distinguished nobleman, Herr von Faninal,	des wohlgeborenen Herrn von Faninal,
Who lives in his palace quite near at hand.	Wohnhaft am "Hof" im eigenen Palais.

(The inn-servants, other guests, and some of the musicians from the other room have crowded round the door and are looking on curiously. Herr von Faninal forces a way through them, hastily attired in hat and coat.)

FANINAL

The same, Sir. What do you wish of me?	Zur Stell'! Was wird von mir gewünscht?

(to the Baron)

How strange you look!	Wie sieht Er aus?
I scarce expected you'd desire my presence	War mir vermutend nicht zu dieser Stunde.
At this untimely hour here in a common pothouse.	In ein gemeines Beisl depeschiert zu werden!

BARON
(very astonished and annoyed)

Why have you stuck your nose in here in the devil's mischief?	Wer hat Ihn hierher depeschiert? In [des] Dreiteufels Namen?

FANINAL
(in an undertone to him)

A damn stupid question indeed, Sir Son-in-law!	Was soll mir die saudumme Frag', Herr Schwiegersohn?
When your excited servants all but broke my door down	Wo Er mir schier die Tür einrennen lässt mit Botschaft,
To tell me I	Ich soll sehr schnell
Must come at once and save you from a horrid situation,	Herbei und Ihn in einer üblen Lage soutenieren
In which, through no fault of yours you had found yourself.	In die Er unverschuld'ter Weise geraten ist!

(The Baron clutches his head.)

COMMISSAR

Who is this man? What is he doing here?	Wer ist der Herr? Was schafft der Herr mit Ihm?

BARON

He's not important, only an acquaintance.	Nichts von Bedeutung. Ist blos ein Bekannter,
Came to this place by sheer coincidence.	hält sich per Zufall hier im Gasthaus auf.

COMMISSAR

Your name, and tell me why you're here!	Der Herr geb' Seinen Namen an!

FANINAL

I am the Baron von Faninal.	Ich in der Edle von Faninal.

COMMISSAR

And this young lady's father?	Somit is dies der Vater . . .

BARON
(coming between them so as to hide Octavian from Faninal. Eagerly)

What he, her father? No, a distant kinsman.	Beileib' gar nicht die Spur. Ist ein Verwandter,
A cousin, it may be. The father is	Ein Bruder, ein Neveu! Der wirkliche
Full twice as fat as he.	Ist noch einmal so dick!

110

FANINAL
(*much astonished*)

What means this, pray? How strange you look. I am her father, surely.

Was geht hier vor? Wie sieht Er aus? Ich bin der Vater, freilich!

BARON
(*trying to draw him aside*)

Now leave it all to me, and get you gone.

Das Weit're findet sich, verzieh' Er sich.

FANINAL

What, you presume, Sir–

Ich muss schon bitten–

BARON

Get you gone, the devil take you.

Fahr' Er heim in Teufels Namen.

FANINAL
(*with growing anger*)

To drag my name into a vulgar brawl in this low tavern! I'll not submit!

Mein Nam' und Ehr' in einen solchen Händel zu melieren, Herr Schwiegersohn!

BARON
(*trying to stop his mouth; to the Commissar*)

It is his fancy.
He calls himself so as a joke.

Ist eine *idée fixe*!
Benennt mich also nur im G'spass!

COMMISSAR

Yes, yes, all right then.

Ja, ja, genügt schon.

(*to Faninal*)

So you recognize
This gentleman as your son-in-law?

Er erkennt demnach
in diesem Herrn [hier] Seinen Schwiegersohn?

FANINAL

Of course, why should I fail to recognize him?
Merely because he's lost his wig?

Sehr wohl! Wieso sollt' ich ihn nicht erkennen?
Leicht weil er keine Haar nicht hat?

COMMISSAR
(*to the Baron*)

And you now recognise this gentleman to be,
For good or evil the young lady's father?

Und Er erkennt nunmehr wohl auch in diesem Herrn
wohl oder übel Seinen Schwiegervater?

BARON
(*taking the candlestick from the table and holding it up to Faninal's face*)

Soso, lala! For all I know that may be so.
This evening I have not been feeling very well.
I can no longer trust my eyes. I must tell you

There's something in this place that gives one apoplectic turns.

Soso, lala! Ja, ja, wird schon derselbe sein.
War heut' den ganzen Abend gar nicht recht beinand'
Kann meinen Augen heut' nicht trau'n. Muss Ihm sagen,
Liegt hier was in der Luft, man kriegt die Congestion davon.

COMMISSAR
(*to Faninal*)

You, on the other hand, admit you are the father
Of this girl here who has been described as

Your daughter?

Dagegen wird von Ihm die Vaterschaft
zu dieser Ihm verbatim zugeschobenen Tochter
Geleugnet?

FANINAL
(*noticing Octavian for the first time*)

As my daughter? That, that baggage,
She says she is a child of mine?

Meine Tochter? Da der Fetzen,
Gibt sich für meine Tochter aus?

BARON
(*with a forced smile*)

A jest! A mere mistake I vow! The landlord

Has told to the Captain of the Watch a tale

Of me, and how I soon shall wed your daughter.

Ein G'spass! Ein purer Missverstand! Der Wirt
Hat dem Herrn kommissarius da was vorerzählt
Von meiner Brautschaft mit der Faninalischen.

111

LANDLORD
(in great excitement)

No word, no word from me, 'twas he there that told the story!	Kein Wort! Kein Wort! Herr Kommissarius Laut eigner Aussag'–

FANINAL
(beside himself)

Arrest that shameless baggage! To the prison!	Das Weibsbild arretieren! Kommt an Pranger!
I'll have her whipped! I'll have her shut up in a convent!	Wird ausgepeitscht! Wird einkastelt in ein Kloster!
I–I–	Ich— ich—

BARON

You'd best go home. Tomorrow I will come	Fahr' Er nach Haus. Auf morgen in der Früh!
And tell you all the truth. You know how much you owe to me.	Ich klär' Ihm alles auf. Er weiss, was Er mir schuldig ist!

FANINAL
(beside himself with rage)

'Twas you that said it!	Laut eig'ner Aussag'!

(taking a few steps to the rear)

Tell my daughter to come here!	Meine Tochter soll herauf!
Her chair is at the doorway! Bid her come at once!	Sitzt unten in der Tragchaise. Im Galopp herauf!

(pouncing on the Baron again)

You'll pay this dearly. I will go to law!	Das zahlt Er teuer! Bring Ihn vor's Gericht!

BARON

What mighty pother you are making now	Jetzt macht Er einen rechten Palawatsch
About a little thing. To be your son-in-law a man must have	Für nichts und wieder nichts! Ein Kavalier braucht ein Rossgeduld,
The patience of an ass, parole d'honneur!	Sein Schwiegersohn zu sein!
Now bring my wig here. Find my wig!	Parole d'honneur! Ich will meine Perücken.

(shaking the Landlord)

Find me my wig!	Meine Perücken will ich seh'n!

(In his wild hunt for his wig, he seizes some of the children and pushes them aside.)

CHILDREN
(automatically)

Papa! Papa! Papa!	Papa! Papa! Papa!

FANINAL
(starting backwards)

Whose brats are these?	Was ist denn das?

BARON

(He succeeds in finding his hat in his search, and hits out at the children with it.)

Nothing! A swindle! I don't know this woman!	Gar nix. Ein Schwindel! Kenn' nit das Bagagi!
She lies, she says that she's my lawful wife.	Si sagt, dass sie verheirat' war mit mir.
Damn it to hell! I am like Daniel in the lions' den.	Käm' zu der Schand' sowie der Pontius ins Credo!

(Sophie hurries in in her coat. They make room for her. Faninal's Footmen can be seen through the door, each with a pole of the chair in his hand. The Baron tries to hide his bald pate from Sophie with his hat, while she goes up to her father.)[44]

ONLOOKERS

The Bride! Oh what a sore disgrace!	Die Braut. Oh was für ein Skandal!

FANINAL
(to Sophie)

Now, look around. See, there your noble suitor stands.	Da schau' dich um! Da hast du den Herrn Bräutigam!
And there his gracious Lordship's family!	Da di Famili von dem saubern Herrn!
The wife and all her children! She's his too,	Die Frau mitsamt die Kinder! Da das Weibsbild.
But a morganatic wife! No, that is you, as he himself has said!	G'hört linker Hand dazu. Nein, das bist du, laut eig'ner Aussag'!
Does not the shame o'erwhelm you? What? Me too.	Möcht'st in die Erd'n sinken, was? Ich auch.

112

SOPHIE
(with a sign of joy)

I'm overjoyed. I never looked on him as mine.	Bin herzensfroh, seh' ihn mit nichten an dafür.

FANINAL

Not look on him as yours? Not look on him as yours?	Sieht ihn nicht an dafür! Sieht ihn nicht an dafür!

(with growing desperation)

My name and fame! I'll be the mock of all the city!	Mein schöner Nam'! Ich trau' mi' nimmer über'n Graben!
I dare not show my face on 'Change again.	Kein Hund nimmt mehr ein Stückl Brot von mir.

(almost in tears)

ONLOOKERS
(by the door, in hollow voices)

The disgrace! The disgrace!	Der Skandal! Der Skandal!
For Herr von Faninal!	Für'n Herrn von Faninal!

FANINAL

[I'll never face the town! The scandal paper!]	[Die ganze Wienerstadt! Die schwarze Zeitung!]
There! From the cellar! From the air! How can I face the town?	Da! Aus dem Keller! Aus der Luft! Die ganze Wienerstadt!

(to the Baron, clenching his fist)

Oh, scoundrel, you! I am not well! A chair!	Oh, Er Filou! Mir wird nicht gut! Ein' Sessel!

(Footmen rush towards him and prevent him from falling. Two of them had previously handed their poles to bystanders. Sophie busies herself about him anxiously. The Landlord also hastens to his aid. They lift him up and carry him into the next room. Several waiters go before them, showing them the way and opening the door. At this moment the Baron catches sight of his wig, which has reappeared as if by magic. He rushes to it, claps it on his head, and sets it straight before a mirror. With this change he regains some of his lost dignity, but he contents himself with turning his back on Annina and the children whose presence makes him uneasy, in spite of everything. The door is closed behind Herr von Faninal and his servants. The Landlord and Waiters soon return quietly, fetch drugs, bottles, water, and other things, which they carry to the door, and Sophie takes them from them in the doorway.)

BARON
(his former self-confidence now completely restored, to the Commissar)

You don't need me any longer. I'll pay, I'll go!	Sind desto eh'r im Klaren. Ich zahl', ich geh'!

(to Octavian)

And now I'll take you home.	Ich führ' Sie jetzt nach Haus.

COMMISSAR

That's where you're wrong. I have some questions for you still.	Da irrt Er sich. Mit Ihm jetzt weiter im Verhör!

(At a sign from the Commissar the two Constables remove the bystanders from the room. Only Annina and the children remain standing by the wall on the left.)

BARON

Leave well alone now, 'twas a jest, I'll tell you later who she truly is.	Lass' Er's jetzt gut sein. War ein G'spass! Ich sag' Ihm später, wer das Mädel is!
I pledge my word: I'll marry her. I tell you in good time.	Geb'Ihm mein Wort, ich heirat' sie wahrscheinlich noch einmal.
The other one in yonder may go hang.	Da hinten dort, das Glumpert is schon stad.
You'll know now what I am and what I am not!	Da sieht Er wer ich bin und wer ich nicht bin!

(about to lead Octavian off)

OCTAVIAN
(shaking him off)

I will not go with him!	I geh' nit mit dem Herrn!

BARON
(in an undertone)

I'll marry you if you keep well with me.	I heirat' Sie, verhält Sie sich mit mir.
So vastly do you please me, you'll be my Baroness!	Sie wird noch Frau Baronin, so gut gefällt Sie mir!

113

OCTAVIAN
(freeing himself from the Baron's grip)

Herr Commissar, I have something to tell you.	Herr Kommissar, i geb' was zu protokoll,
But out of the hearing of the Baron.	Aber der Herr Baron darf nicht zuhör'n dabei.

(At a sign from the Commissar, the two Constables force the Baron to the front right. Octavian seems to be telling the Commissar something which surprises him very much. The Commissar accompanies Octavian to the alcove. Octavian disappears behind the curtains.)
[43]

BARON
(aside to the Constables, in a familiar tone, pointing to Annina)

God knows who she may be, I swear. We were at supper.	Kenn' nicht das Weibsbild dort, auf Ehr'. War grad beim Essen!
I've not a notion what she wants, else I would never call on you for help.	Hab' keine Ahnung, was es will. Hätt' sonst nicht selber an die Polizei–

(The Commissar seems to be much entertained, and approaches the curtain without concern.)

BARON
(noticing the Commissar's amusement; suddenly much excited by the strange incident)

What's happening there? Can it be possible? The villain!	Was g'schiet denn dort? Ist wohl nicht möglich das? Der Lackl!
No, no, he can't do that to me! She is a maiden! She is a virgin!	Das heisst Ihr Sittenpolizei? Ist eine Jungfer!

(He is restrained with difficulty.)

I am her guardian, as you see. I warn you.	Steht unter meiner Protektion! Beschwer' mich!
You will pay for this behaviour!	Hab' [da] ein Wörtel drein zu reden!

(He frees himself, and goes towards the recess. They pursue him and seize him again. Mariandel's clothes are thrown out of the recess, piece by piece. The Commissar makes a bundle of them. The Baron struggles with his two captors. They have much trouble in holding him, when Octavian's head appears at the opening of the curtains.)

You'd better let me go.	Muss jetzt partout zu ihr.

LANDLORD
(rushing in)

Gentlemen, Her Serene Highness, the Princess von Werdenberg!	Ihre hochfürstliche Gnaden, die Frau Fürstin Feldmarschallin!

(Enter first servants in the Marschallin's livery, then the Baron's Body Servant. They form a line. Enter the Marschallin, the little Black Boy carrying her train.) [5]

BARON
(He has freed himself from the Constables, and wiping the perspiration from his brow, hurries over to the Marschallin.)

I'm glad beyond all measure. This is more than I deserve.	Bin glücklich über Massen, hab' die Gnad' kaum meritiert,
Your intervention here shows me a kindness quite unequalled.	Schätz' Dero Gegenwart hier als ein Freundstück ohne Gleichen.

OCTAVIAN
(putting his head out from between the curtains) [1]

Marie Theres', how come you here?	Marie Theres', wie kommt Sie her?

(The Marschallin stands motionless, not answering. She looks round with a questioning glance. The Body Servant, proud and pleased with himself, goes up to the Baron. The Baron indicates his satisfaction with him.)

COMMISSAR
(going towards the Marschallin, at attention)

May't please Your Highness, your most humble servant,	Fürstliche Gnaden, melde mich gehorsamst
The Commissary of the district.	Als vorstads Unterkommissarius.

BARON
(at the same time)

You see, Herr Kommissar, Her Highness comes in person to my aid.	Er sieht, Herr Kommissar, die Durchlaut haben selber sich bemüht.
You see with whom you have to deal.	Ich denk', Er weiss, woran Er ist.

MARSCHALLIN
(*to the Commissar, paying no attention to the Baron*)

You know me? And I think I know you too? I think I do.

Er kennt mich? Kenn' ich Ihn nicht auch? Mir scheint beinah'.

COMMISSAR

Yes, well!

Sehr wohl!

MARSCHALLIN

I remember now, you were my husband's orderly?

Dem Herrn Feldmarschall sein' brave Ordonanz gewest?

COMMISSAR

Yes, Your Highness, to command!

Fürstliche Gnaden, zu Befehl!

(*Octavian again pops his head through the curtains.*)

BARON
(*Signalling to Octavian to disappear, at the same time in great anxiety lest the Marschallin should notice anything. In an undertone.*)

Stay there confound you, out of sight!

Bleib' Sie, zum Sakra, hinten dort!

(*He hears steps approaching the door on the left to the front, rushes there, and places himself with his back to the door, trying, by means of deferential gestures in the Marschallin's direction, to appear quite at ease. The Marschallin steps over to the left, and looks at the Baron expectantly.*)

OCTAVIAN
(*Coming from behind the curtains in male clothing, as soon as the Baron has turned his back.*)

Our plan has gone astray, Marie Theres', so strangely.

War anders abgemacht! Marie Theres', ich wunder mich!

(*The Marschallin ignores Octavian, and fixes a courteous and expectant look on the Baron, who is dividing his attention, in the utmost perplexity, between the Marschallin and the door. The door on the left is violently opened, so that the Baron, who had been leaning against it in a vain attempt to keep it closed, is forced back. Two of Faninal's servants now stand aside to let Sophie pass.*)

SOPHIE
(*not seeing the Marschallin, who is hidden by the Baron*)

My father, Sir, has bidden me inform you—

Hab' Ihm von mei'm Herrn Vater zu vermelden—

BARON
(*interrupting her, in an undertone*)

Oh, fiddlesticks, my girl, I have no time! Will you not wait until I come and call for you? Can you suppose that I'd present you in a brothel here?

Ist jetzo nicht die Zeit, Kreuzelement! Kann Sie nicht warten, bis dass man Ihr rufen wird? Meint Sie, dass ich Sie hier im Beisl präsentieren werd'?

OCTAVIAN
(*who now comes quietly forward from the alcove, in an undertone to the Marschallin*)

That is the lady, she, to whom you sent me—

Das ist die Fräulein—die— um derentwillen—

MARSCHALLIN
(*to Octavian, over her shoulder, in an undertone*)

You seem a little too concerned, Rofrano. Who she is I can surely guess. She has great charm.

Find' Ihn ein Bissl empressiert, Rofrano. Kann mir wohl denken, wer sie ist. Find' sie charmant.

(*Octavian slips back between the curtains.*)

SOPHIE
(*with her back to the door, so angrily that the Baron instinctively starts back a step*) [24]

I must inform Your Lordship you'll present me to no-one. For I would have you know I have done with you, once and for all.

Er wird mich keinem Menschen auf der Welt nicht präsentieren, Dieweilen ich mit Ihm auch nicht *so* viel zu schaffen hab'.

(*The Marschallin converses in a low tone with the Commissar.*)

And this my father bids me tell you: should you carry your

Und mein Herr Vater lässt Ihm sagen: wenn Er alsoweit

Unmannerly presumption only just so far
As to be seen within a hundred yards of where our palace stands,
You'll have yourself alone to thank for what will then befall you.
That, Sir, is what my father bids me to say to you.

Die Frechheit sollte treiben, dass man Seine Nasen nur
Erblicken tät' auf hundert Schritt von unserm Stadtpalais,
So hätt' Er sich die bösen Folgen selber zuzuschreiben.
Das ist's, was mein Herr Vater Ihm vermelden lässt.

BARON
(*angrily*)
Corpo di Bacco!
What a shocking use of disrespectful language!

Corpo di Bacco!
Was ist das für eine ungezogene Sprache?

SOPHIE
To match your own.

Die Ihm gebührt.

BARON
(*beside himself, trying to pass her and reach the door*)
Hey, Faninal, I must–

He Faninal, ich muss–

SOPHIE
Stand back, Sir. Do not dare!

Er untersteh' sich nicht!

(*Faninal's two Footmen come forward, bar his passage, and push him back. Sophie passes through the door, which is closed behind her.*)

BARON
(*shouting through the door*)
I'm willing to forget what's happened.
I'll let it be forgiven and forgotten.

Bin willens, alles Vorgefall'ne
Vergeben und vergessen sein zu lassen!

MARSCHALLIN
(*approaching the Baron from behind, and tapping him on the shoulder.*)
Leave well alone now; and go quickly. At once now.

Lass'Er nur gut sein und verschwind' Er auf eins, zwei!

BARON
(*turning round and staring at her*)
But madam,

Wieso denn?

MARSCHALLIN
(*gaily, sure of victory*)
Think of your dignity and take your leave!　Wahr'Er Sein Dignité und fahr' Er ab!

BARON
(*speechless*)
I? How?

Ich? Was?

MARSCHALLIN
Make your "bonne mine à mauvais jeu".
And make your exit nobly, like a gentleman.

Mach 'Er bonne mine à mauvais jeu;
So bleibt Er quasi doch noch eine Standsperson.

(*The Baron stares at her in amazement. Enter Sophie from the other room, quietly. Her eyes seek Octavian.*)

MARSCHALLIN
(*to the Commissar who is standing at the back on the right with the two Constables*)
You see, Herr Kommissar,
This all has been just a diversion, and nothing more.

Er sieht, Herr Kommissar:
das ganze war halt eine Farce und weiter nichts.

COMMISSAR
Alright then. Respectfully I leave you.

Genügt mir! Retirier' mich ganz gehorsamst.

(*Exit, followed by the two Constables*)

SOPHIE
(*aside, frightened*)
This all has been just a diversion and nothing more.

Das ganze war halt eine Farce und weiter nichts.

(*The eyes of the two women meet; Sophie makes an embarrassed curtsey.*)

BARON
(*standing between Sophie and the Marschallin*)
Don't understand it!

Bin gar nicht willens!

MARSCHALLIN

(impatiently stamping her foot)

Now cousin, explain to him.   Mon cousin, bedeut' Er Ihm!

(She turns her back on the Baron.)

OCTAVIAN

(approaching the Baron from behind, in a very masculine manner)

Will you permit me?   Möcht' Ihn sehr bitten!

BARON

(turning sharply towards him)

Who? What?   Wer? Was?

MARSCHALLIN

(from the right, where she has now taken up her position)

Your Lordship, this is Count Rofrano, who   Sein' Gnaden, der Herr Graf **Rofrano**, wer
then else?   denn sonst?

BARON

(resignedly, after carefully studying Octavian's face)

Just as I thought.   Is schon a so!

(aside)

That face it makes me sick.   Hab' g'nug von dem Gesicht,
My eyes did not deceive me then.   Sind doch nicht meine Augen schuld.
It was that boy, then.   Is schon ein Mandl.

(Octavian stands there looking insolent and defiant.)

MARSCHALLIN

(coming one step closer)

It was a harmless little masquerade and   Is eine wienerische Maskerad' und **weiter**
nothing else.   nichts.

SOPHIE

(aside, half sad, half ironically)

It was a harmless little masquerade and   Is eine wienerische Maskerad' und **weiter**
nothing more.   nichts.

BARON

(dumbfounded)

Aha!   Aha!

(aside)

I see now they were all conspiring to defeat   Spiel'n alle unter einem Leder gegen
me!   meiner!

MARSCHALLIN

(haughtily)

'Tis well for you it was not   Ich hätt' Ihm nicht gewunschen,
Really my Mariandl whom you brought   Dass Er mein Mariandl in der Wirklichkeit
into this place here to seduce.   mir hätte debauchiert!

(The Baron is deep in thought as the Marschallin continues, without looking at Octavian.)

I feel, just now against all men such a [5] Hab' jetzt einen montierten Kopf gegen die
resentment—   Männer—
Against all men in general!   so ganz im Allgemeinen!

BARON

(gradually realizing the situation)

Well I'll be damned! Now I begin to see it   Kreuzelement! Komm' aus dem Staunen
all!   nicht heraus!
The Feldmarschall—Octavian—   Der Feldmarschall—Octavian—
Mariandl—the Marschallin—Octavian—   Mariandl—die Marschallin—Octavian—

*(with a comprehensive glance, which wanders from the Marschallin to Octavian, and
from Octavian back to the Marschallin)*

How should I know what I, in my confusion,   Weiss bereits nicht, was ich von diesem
am supposed   ganzem qui pro quo
To think of this!   [6]   mir denken soll!

MARSCHALLIN

(looking at him fixedly, then more emphatically)

You are surely a cavalier? So you will just   Er ist, mein' ich, ein Kavalier? Da wird Er
refrain from thinking.   sich halt gar nichts denken.
That is what I expect from you.   Das ist's, was ich von Ihm erwart'!

BARON
(bowing with the grace of a man of the world)

I am simply delighted and charmed, beyond description charmed.	Bin von so viel Finesse charmiert, kann gar nicht sagen, wie.
No Lerchenauer ever had the heart to spoil a joke.	Ein Lerchenauer war noch nie kein Spielverderber nicht.

(coming one step nearer)

I like the way you've played this comedy,	Find' deliziös das ganze qui-pro-quo,
But now I must demand you intercede on my behalf.	Bedarf aber dafür nunmehro Ihrer Protektion.
I promise to be discreet about it all.	Bin willens, alles Vorgefallene
I'll let it be forgiven and forgotten.	Vergeben und vergessen sein zu lassen.

(pause)

Eh bien, may I tell Faninal—	Eh bien, darf ich den Faninal—

(going to the left-hand door)

MARSCHALLIN

You may—you may without a word withdraw and leave us.	Er darf—Er darf in aller Still' sich retirieren.

(The Baron is dumbfounded.)

Can you not tell when an affair is ended? [20]	Versteht Er nicht, wenn eine Sach' ein End'hat?
Your talk of marriage, that affair, and everything	Die ganze Brautschaft und Affär' und alles sonst,
Connected with it	Was drum und dran hängt,

(very emphatically)

From this hour is at an end.	ist mit dieser Stund' vorbei.

SOPHIE

Connected with it, from this hour is at an end.	Was drum und dran hängt, ist mit dieser Stund' vorbei.

BARON
(aside, very indignant, softly)

Is at an end, an end! Is at an end, an end!	Mit dieser Stund' vorbei! Mit dieser Stund' vorbei!

MARSCHALLIN
(She seems to be looking for a seat. Octavian hurries forward and gives her a chair. The Marschallin sits down on the right. Aside, in a significant tone.)

Is at an end. [5]	Ist halt vorbei.

SOPHIE
(on the left, aside, pale)

Is at an end.	Ist halt vorbei.

(The Baron fails to appreciate this new development, and rolls his eyes in anger and perplexity. At this moment the man emerges from the trapdoor. Valzacchi enters from the left, followed by his suspicious accomplices, with modest demeanour. Annina tears off her widow's cap and veil, rubs off her make-up, revealing her natural face. The Baron's astonishment grows. The Landlord enters by the centre door, carrying a long bill, followed by waiters, musicians, house boys, and coachmen.)

BARON
(As he sees them, he realizes that the game is lost. He calls out quickly and decidedly.)

Leopold, we go.	Leopold, wir geh'n!

(He makes a low, angry bow to the Marschallin. His Body Servant seizes a candle from the table, and prepares to lead the way for his master. Annina insolently bars the Baron's passage.)

ANNINA

"I still have all the luck of the Lerchenaus." [33]	"Ich hab' halt schon einmal ein Lerchenauisch Glück."

(pointing to the Landlord's bill)

"Come when I've dined, I'll give the answer in writing." [31]	"Komm' Sie nach Tisch, geb' Ihr die Antwort nachher schriftlich!"

(The Children run between the Baron's legs. He hits out at them with his hat.)

CHILDREN

Papa! Papa! Papa!	Papa! Papa! Papa!

WAITERS
(pressing forward to the Baron)

May't please you, Your Highness! [37]	Entschuld'gen Euer Gnaden!

There are lights to pay!   Uns geh'n die Kerzen an!

LANDLORD
(pressing forward with his bill)
May't please you, Your Highness! ·   Entschuld'gen Euer Gnaden!

ANNINA
(dancing backwards in front of the Baron)
"I still have all the luck of the Lerchenaus."   "Ich hab' halt schon einmal ein
                                            Lerchenauisch Glück!"

VALZACCHI
(ironically)
"I still have all the luck of the Lerchenaus!"   "Ich hab' halt schon einmal ein
                                            Lerchenauisch Glück!"

MUSICIANS
(barring the Baron's passage)
There's music, two hours and more, Sir.   Tafelmusik über zwei Stunden!
(The Body Servant forces a way to the door; the Baron tries to follow him.)

COACHMEN
(crowding round the Baron)
For the coach, for the coach. Horses   Für die Fuhr', für die Fuhr'! Rösser
standing. Time is up!   g'schund'n ham ma g'nua!

BOOTS
(insolently bawling at the Baron)
Don't forget, Sir, I lock the house.   Sö für's Aufsperr'n, Sö, Herr Baron.

LANDLORD
(still presenting his bill)
May't please you, Your Lordship.   Entschuld'gen Euer Gnaden!

WAITERS
Two score candles. There are the lights to   Zwei Schock Kerzen, uns geh'n die Kerzen
pay.   an!

BARON
(in the crowd)
Way there, way there, out of my way!   Platz da, zurück da, Kreuzmillion!

BOOTS
I help the coachman, Sir, I lock the house.   Führa g'fahr'n, aussa g'ruckt, Sö, Herr
                                      Baron!

CHILDREN
Papa! Papa! Papa!   Papa! Papa! Papa!

(All shout in wild confusion. They reach the door. The candle is wrested from the Body Servant. The Baron rushes off; all hurry after him. The noise grows fainter. Faninal's two Footmen have gone out by the door on the left. Sophie, the Marschallin, and Octavian are left alone.)

SOPHIE
(standing on the left, pale)
Oh God! The story was a masquerade and   Mein Gott, es war nicht mehr als eine Farce.
no more.
Oh God!   Mein Gott! Mein Gott!
He goes towards her, and I am no more   Wie Er bei Ihr steht und ich bin die leere
alive for him.   Luft für ihn.

OCTAVIAN
(behind the Marschallin's chair, embarassed)
Our plan has gone astray, Marie Therese,   War anders abgemacht, Marie Theres', ich
so strangely!   wunder'mich.
(in extreme embarassment)
Command me, shall I—should I not—the   Befiehlt Sie, dass ich—soll ich nicht—die
Lady—her father—   Jungfer—der Vater—

MARSCHALLIN
Go quickly, and do all that your heart   Geh' Er doch schnell und tu' Er, was Sein
commands.   Herz Ihm sagt.

SOPHIE
(in despair)
No more alive! Oh my God! Ah God!   Die leere Luft, O mein Gott, O mein Gott!

119

| | **OCTAVIAN** | |
| Therese, I do not know— | | Theres', ich weiss gar nicht— |

| | **MARSCHALLIN** | |
| Go now, and pay her your court. | | Geh' Er und mach' Er Seinen Hof. |

| | **OCTAVIAN** | |
| I swear it— | | Ich schwör' Ihr— |

| | **MARSCHALLIN** | |
| 'Tis no matter. | | Lass'Er's gut sein. |

| | **OCTAVIAN** | |
| But I do not understand. | | Ich begreif' nicht, was Sie hat. |

MARSCHALLIN
(*laughing angrily*)

| How like a man to say that. Go to her! | | Er ist ein rechtes Mannsbild, geh'Er hin. |

OCTAVIAN

| As you command. | | Was Sie befiehlt. |

(*He goes to her. Sophie stands speechless*)

| Eh bien, have you no friendly word for me? | | [45] Eh bien, hat Sie kein freundlich Wort für mich? |
| No glance or smile, no smile to show that you care? | | Nicht einen Blick, nicht einen lieben Gruss? |

SOPHIE
(*hesitating*)

| Ah, my Lord, I had dared to expect of you and your chivalry | | War mir von Euer Gnaden Freundschaft und Behilflichkeit |
| A token of affection more than pity. | | Wahrhaftig einer andern Freud' gewärtig. |

OCTAVIAN
(*eagerly*)

| What? Are you not then glad? | | Wie—freut Sie sich denn nicht? |

SOPHIE
(*angrily*)

| Pray, then tell me what cause I have. | | Hab' wirklich keinen Anlass nicht. |

OCTAVIAN

| Have we not chased that wretch away that made you sad? | | Hat man Ihr nicht den Bräutigam vom Hals geschafft? |

SOPHIE

It could have been a day of happiness and joy.		Wär' all's recht schön, wenn's anders abgegangen wär'.
Yet all conspires to shame me. And in the smile		Schäm' mich in Grund und Boden [jetzt]. Versteh' sehr wohl
Her Highness turns on me I can feel all the pity and the scorn.		Mit was für einem Blick Ihre fürstliche Gnaden mich betracht'.

OCTAVIAN

| I swear upon my soul it is not so! | | Ich schwör' Ihr meiner Seel' und Seligkeit. |

SOPHIE

| Pray let me go now! | | Lass' Er mich geh'n. |

OCTAVIAN

| I never shall! | | Ich lass' Sie nicht. |

(*seizing her hand*)

SOPHIE

| My father needs my help. | | Der Vater braucht mich drin. |

OCTAVIAN

| I need you more than he! | | Ich brauch' Sie nötiger. |

SOPHIE

| 'Tis lightly said. | | Das sagt sich leicht. |

(*The Marschallin rises abruptly, but controls herself, and sits down again.*)

OCTAVIAN

| I love you more than words can say. | | Ich hab' Sie übermässig lieb. |

SOPHIE

It is not true.		Das ist nicht wahr,
Your love is not as great as you declare.		Er hat mich nicht so lieb, als wie Er spricht.
Forget me then!		Vergess' Er mich!

	OCTAVIAN
You are my all, you are my all!	Ist mir um Sie und nur um Sie!

	SOPHIE
Forget me then!	Vergess' Er mich!

OCTAVIAN
(*vehemently*)

The world may vanish for all I care!	Mag Alles drunter oder drüber geh'n!

SOPHIE
(*passionately*)

Forget me then!	Vergess' Er mich!

	OCTAVIAN
My hopes are fastened on you alone.	Hab' keinen andern Gedanken nicht,
I'm blinded to all but your face.	Seh' alleweil Ihr lieb Gesicht.

(*taking both her hands in his*)

SOPHIE
(*weakly pushing him away*)

Forget me then!	Vergess'Er mich!

MARSCHALLIN
(*aside, at the same time*)

Now or tomorrow, if not tomorrow, very soon,	Heut' oder morgen oder den übernächsten Tag.
Did I not say the words myself?	Hab' ich mir's denn nicht vorgesagt?
There is no woman can escape this fate.	Das alles kommt halt über jede Frau.
Did I not know the truth?	Hab' ich's den nicht gewusst?
Did I not take a vow on it?	Hab' ich nicht ein Gelübde tan,
That I with all my heart must be humble	Dass ich's mit einem ganz gefassten Herzen
And bear the blow...	Ertragen werd'...
Now or tomorrow, if not tomorrow, very soon.	Heut' oder morgen oder den übernächsten Tag.

(*She wipes her eyes and stands up.*)

SOPHIE
(*softly*)

Her Ladyship! She's calling you! Go speak to her!	Die Fürstin da! Sie ruft Ihn hin. So geh' Er doch!

(*Octavian takes a few steps towards the Marschallin, and stands in indecision between the two. Pause. Sophie, in the doorway, cannot decide whether to stay or go. Octavian between them turns his head from one to the other. The Marschallin notices his perplexity and a melancholy smile flits across her face.*)

I must go in, I think I hear my father call.	Ich muss hinein und fragen, wie's dem Vater geht.

	OCTAVIAN
So much is unspoken, I have no words to speak.	Ich muss jetzt was reden, und mir verschlagt's die Red'.

	MARSCHALLIN
Poor boy, look how confused he stands there between us two.	Der Bub, wie er verlegen da in der Mitten steht!

OCTAVIAN
(*to Sophie*)

By all that's holy, stay.	Bleib' Sie um Alles hier.

(*to the Marschallin*)

Yes. What was that you said?	Wie, hat Sie was gesagt?

MARSCHALLIN
(*She pays no attention to Octavian, but crosses over to Sophie and looks at her critically but kindly. Sophie curtsies in embarrassment.*)

So quickly have you learned to love him?	[5] So schnell hat Sie ihn gar so lieb?

SOPHIE
(*very quickly*)

Indeed, Ma'am, your question I can hardly understand.	Ich weiss nicht, was Euer Gnaden meinen mit der Frag'.

	MARSCHALLIN
Your cheek so pale gives me the answer plain enough.	Ihr blass' Gesicht gibt schon die rechte Antwort d'rauf.

(very timid and embarassed. Still very quickly)

No wonder if my cheeks are pale, Your Highness.	Wär' gar kein Wunder, wenn ich blass bin, Euer Gnaden,
I have been dreadfully afraid for my poor father,	Hab' einen grossen Schreck erlebt mit dem Herrn Vater.
Not to speak also of my anger at all the vile things that that hateful man has said and done.	Gar nicht zu reden von gerechtem Emportement gegen den skandalösen Herrn Baron.
I am most grateful, forever grateful to Your Highness for your help and kindness.	Bin Euer Gnaden in Ewigkeit verpflichtet Dass mit Dero Hilf' und Aufsicht—

MARSCHALLIN

(deprecatingly)

No need to talk so much. You're pretty, that's enough!	Red' Sie nur nicht zu viel, Sie ist ja hübsch genug!
And as for your dear Papa's discomfort, I know just the medicine for him.	Und gegen dem Herrn Papa sein übel, weiss ich etwa eine Medizin.
I'll go, say a few words to him, and bid him	Ich geh' jetzt da hinein zu ihm und lad' ihn ein,
Drive with me and you and Count Octavian in my own carriage home beside me— don't you think	mit mir und Ihr und dem Herrn Grafen da, in meinem Wagen heimzufahren— meint Sie nicht,
That will be quite enough to make him well again	Dass ihn das recreieren wird und allbereits
And even cheer his spirits?	Ein wenig munter machen?

SOPHIE

Ah, Your Highness, you are much too kind.	Euer Gnaden sind die Güte selbst.

MARSCHALLIN

And for your pale cheeks, I think my cousin there will know the cure.	Und für die Blässe weiss vielleicht mein Vetter da die Medizin.

OCTAVIAN

(with deep feeling)

Marie Therese, how good you are.	Marie Theres', wie gut Sie ist.
Marie Therese, I do not know—	Marie Theres', ich weiss gar nicht—

MARSCHALLIN

(with an enigmatic expression, softly)

I know nothing—	Ich weiss auch nix.

(quite without expression)

Nothing.	Gar nix.

(She indicates to him to stay)

OCTAVIAN

(undecided, as if he wished to follow her)

Marie Therese!	Marie Theres'!

(The Marschallin remains standing in the door. Octavian is beside her, Sophie further off to the right.)

MARSCHALLIN

(aside, at the same time as Octavian and Sophie)

I made a vow to love him rightly, as a [46] good woman should,	Hab' mir's gelobt, ihn liebzuhaben in der richtigen Weis',
E'en to love the love he bore another,	Dass ich selbst sein Lieb' zu einer andern
I promised. But in truth, I did not think	noch lieb hab'! Hab' mir freilich nicht gedacht,
That all so soon I'd find the task await me.	dass es so bald mir auferlegt sollt' werden!

(sighing)

Full many a thing is ordained in this world,	Es sind die mehreren Dinge auf der Welt,
Which we should scarce believe could be	So dass sie ein's nicht glauben tät',
If we heard others tell of them.	Wenn man sie möcht' erzählen hör'n.
And only we who live them believe in them, and know not how—	Alleinig wer's erlebt, der glaubt daran und weiss nicht wie—
There stands the boy, and here stand I, and with this pretty child of his	Da steht der Bub und da steh' ich, und mit dem fremden Mädel dort
He will know happiness such as a man thinks	Wird er so glücklich sein, als wie halt Männer

The best the world can give. Well then, so be it.

Das Glücklichsein verstehen. In Gottes Namen.

OCTAVIAN
(together with the Marschallin and Sophie, first to himself, then gazing into Sophie's eyes)

Can I believe it has come to pass?	Es ist was kommen und ist was g'scheh'n.
Would I could ask her, 'Can it be?' And just that question	Ich möcht' Sie fragen: Darf's denn sein? und g'rad' die Frag',
Is the question that I dare not ask.	Die spür' ich, dass Sie mir verboten ist
Would I could ask her, why, oh why, am I so afraid?	Ich möcht' Sie fragen: Warum zittert was in mir?—
What if a cruel wrong has been done? And yet of her	Ist denn ein grosses Unrecht g'scheh'n? Und grad an die
I may not ask the question—and then I see you by me,	Darf' ich die Frag' nicht tun—und dann seh' ich dich an,
Sophie, and see but you, know but you,	Sophie, und seh' nur dich und spür' nur dich,
Sophie, and know no more but you: you, you I love.	Sophie, und weiss von nichts als nur: dich hab' ich lieb.

SOPHIE
(together with the Marschallin and Octavian, at first to herself, then gazing into Octavian's eyes)

I feel as when I'm kneeling, holy rapture mixed with fear,	Mir ist wie in der Kirch'n, heilig ist mir und so bang,
And rapture that's unholy too, I know not what I feel.	Und doch ist mir unheilig auch! Ich weiss nicht, wie mir ist.

(with much expression)

I'd gladly kneel before my Lady there, yet I'd hurt her	Ich möcht' mich niederknie'n dort vor der Frau und möcht' ihr [auch]
Gladly; for I feel, she gives me him,	Was antun, denn ich spür', sie gibt mir ihn
And yet robs me of part of him.	Und nimmt mir was von ihm zugleich.
I know not how it is!	Weiss gar nicht wie mir ist!
Could I understand! And yet I fear the truth!	Möcht' alls verstehen und möcht' auch nichts verstehen.
I would know and yet not know; I am hot and cold.	Möcht fragen und nicht fragen, wird heiss und kalt.
And know but you, know but this one thing: that I love you.	Und spür' nur dich und weiss nur eins: dich hab' ich lieb!

(The Marschallin goes quietly into the room on the left; the two others do not notice her. Octavian comes close to Sophie. A moment later she is in his arms.)

OCTAVIAN

Bliss too deep to understand,	[47] Spür' nur dich, spür' nur dich allein
One in happiness and hand in hand!	Und dass wir beieinander sein!
Years to come glimmer like the sun	Geht all's sonst wie ein Traum dahin
Before my eyes!	Vor meinem Sinn!

SOPHIE

Am I dreaming that here we stand,	Ist ein Traum, kann nicht wirklich sein,
One in happiness and hand in hand?	Dass wir zwei beieinander sein,
Ever hand in hand to be	Beieinand' für alle Zeit
For all eternity!	Und Ewigkeit!

OCTAVIAN

In a palace once upon a day,	War ein Haus wo, da warst du drein
You were waiting till I stole you away	Und die Leute schicken mich hinein,
They let me steal the brightest jewel there,	Mich gradaus in die Seligkeit!
Fools that they were!	Die waren g'scheidt!

SOPHIE

You are laughing? I stand in dread	Kannst du lachen? Mir ist zur Stell'
Such a tumult runs in my head.	Bang wie an der himmlischen Schwell'!
Hold me! A weak foolish thing	Halt mich, ein schwach Ding wie ich bin,
To you I cling!	Sink' dir dahin!

(She leans on him for support. At this moment Faninal's Footmen open the door and enter, each carrying a candlestick. Faninal, leading the Marschallin by the hand, enters through the door. The two young people stand for a moment in confusion, then they make a deep bow, which Faninal and the Marschallin return. Faninal pats Sophie on the cheek with paternal benevolence.)

123

	FANINAL
'Tis ever so, youth will be youth!	Sind halt aso, die jungen Leut'!
	MARSCHALLIN
Ah, yes.	Ja, ja.

Faninal gives the Marschallin his hand, and conducts her to the centre door, which is at that moment thrown open by the Marschallin's suite, among them the little Black Boy. Outside the light is bright, inside it is half-dark, as the two Footmen precede the Marschallin with the candlesticks. Octavian and Sophie are left alone in the darkened room. Dreamily they repeat:

OCTAVIAN

Bliss too deep to understand,	Spür' nur dich, spür' nur dich allein
One in happiness and hand in hand!	Und dass wir beieinander sein!
Years to come glimmer like the sun	[29] Geht all's sonst wie ein Traum dahin
Before my eyes!	Vor meinem Sinn!

SOPHIE

Am I dreaming that here we stand,	Ist ein Traum, kann nicht wirklich sein,
One in happiness and hand in hand?	Dass wir zwei beieinander sein,
Ever hand in hand to be	Beieinand' für alle Zeit
For all eternity!	Und Ewigkeit!

She sinks into his arms. He kisses her quickly. Her handkerchief drops from her hand without her noticing. Then they run quickly off, hand in hand. The stage remains empty. Then the centre door opens again. The little Black Boy comes in with a taper in his hand, looks for the handkerchief, finds it, and trips out. [9]

The curtain falls slowly.

Two designs for Act Three. Above: the 'art nouveau' design by Luchino Visconti and Ferdinando Scarfiotti for Covent Garden. (photo: Donald Southern)

Opposite. Erté's design for Glyndebourne, 1980, in John Cox's production, set around 1850. (© Sevenarts Limited; by courtesy of Erté and the Grosvenor Gallery)

Bibliography

Perceptive discussions of *Der Rosenkavalier* are contained in the major studies in English of Richard Strauss: Norman del Mar's *Richard Strauss: A critical commentary on his life and works* (Barrie and Rockliff, 3 volumes, 1962–1972; reprinted with corrections, 1978) and William Mann's *Richard Strauss: A Critical Study of the Operas* (Cassell, 1964). Michael Kennedy's volume on the composer for the *Master Musician* series (Dent, 1976) is the best short introduction to his total output. The fascinating correspondence between Strauss and Hofsmannsthal (Collins, 1961; reprinted Cambridge U. P., 1981) is a unique record of the collaboration of a composer and librettist. Alan Jefferson has published several books on Strauss notably *The Life of Richard Strauss* (David & Charles, 1973) and *Richard Strauss* (Macmillan, 1975).

Discography Available recordings in stereo (unless asterisked*) and in German. Cassette tape numbers are also given. A valuable review of all performances on record by Alan Jefferson is contained in *Opera on Record* (ed. Alan Blyth, Hutchinson 1979)

Conductor	Szell	Kleiber	Karajan
Company/Orchestra	VPO	Vienna Opera VPO	Philharmonia
Marschallin	Reiner	M. Reining	E. Schwarzkopf
Ochs	Prohaska	L. Weber	O. Edelmann
Octavian	Novotna	S. Jurinac	C. Ludwig
Faninal	Hann	A. Poell	E. Waechter
Sophie	H. Gueden	H. Gueden	T. Stich-Randall
Leitmetzerin			L. Welitsch
Valzacchi	Klein	P. Klein	P. Kuen
Annina	Hermann	H. Rössl-Majdan	K. Meyer
Commissar			A. Bierbach
Singer	Roswaenge	A. Dermota	N. Gedda
Disc UK number	L096/4	4BB 115–8	SLS 810
Tape UK number			SLS 810
Excerpts (Disc)			
Excerpts (Tape)			
Disc US number			S3563
Tape US number			
Excerpts (Disc) US			S35645

| *Böhm* | *Solti* | *de Waart* | *Bernstein* |
Dresden State Opera	**VPO**	**Netherlands Op. Rotterdam PO**	**Vienna Opera VPO**
M. Schech	R. Crespin	E. Lear	C. Ludwig
K. Boehme	M. Jungwirth	J. Bastin	W. Berry
I. Seefried	Y. Minton	F. von Stade	G. Jones
D. Fischer-Dieskau	O. Wiener	D. Hammond-Stroud	Gutstein
R. Streich	H. Donath	R. Welting	L. Popp
I. Steingruber	E. Loose		
G. Unger	M. Dickie	J. Atherton	M. Dickie
S. Wagner	A. Howells	S. van Sante	Lilowa
A. Peter	H. Lackner	H. Smit	
R. Franci	L. Pavarotti	J. Carreras	P. Domingo
2721 162	**SET 418–21**	**6707030**	
K3 N23	**7699 045**		
	SET 487		
	KCET 487		
	1435	**6707030**	**D4M–30652**
	5–1435	**7699045**	
	262000		**M–31959**

Excerpts

Number	Artists	Disc Number	Tape Number
Highlights	L. Lehmann/M. Olszewska/R. Mayr/ E. Schumann/VPO/Heger	SH 181–2*	
Highlights	R. Crespin/E. Söderström/Holecek/H. Gueden/ VPO/Varviso	JB 57	KJBC 57
Di rigori armato	L. Pavarotti	SXL 6658	KSXC 6658
Di rigori armato	L. Pavarotti	D129 D2	K129 K22
Da geht er hin/Die Zeit im Grunde	A. Varnay	DE22 645*	
Herr Gott in Himmel	E. Scharzkopf/I. Seefried/VPO/Karajan	SH 286*	
Da lieg ich	D. Hermann/L. Weber/VPO/Ackermann	SH 286	
Letter scene	A. Kipnis/E. Ruzicka	SH 280*	
Letter scene	M. Langdon/Y. Minton	SET 392–3	
Orchestral excerpts	LPO/del Mar	CFP 40327	